Caribbean History

A Captivating Guide to the History of the West Indies and the Golden Age of Piracy

Table of Contents

Part 1: History of the Caribbean

A Captivating Guide to Caribbean History, Starting from Christopher Columbus through the Wars of Religion, Slavery, and Colonial Laws to the Present

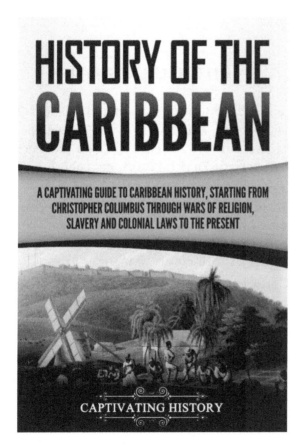

Introduction

The Caribbean has over seven thousand islands. Thirteen are sovereign nations, with some still subjects of their parent nations. Over the last five hundred years, the region has been the site of impactful events, creating a rich history and culture.

In the beginning, the Taíno people settled there, with many living in separate tribes. Their history before the pre-colonial era is unknown, so we only have guesses as to where they came from. But their presence was confirmed through the discovery of European explorers and, later, the discovery of many artifacts.

When Christopher Columbus inadvertently discovered the Caribbean, he mistook the region for Asia. However, it opened up new opportunities for European nations. Through the years, Spain would dominate the region before going to war with other nations, such as France and England.

Spain continued to maintain its claim over many nations in the Caribbean until the late 19th century, when it surrendered many of its territories to other countries, including France, the United States, and others.

Today, some European nations still claim parts of the Caribbean. The nation of Curaçao in the Lesser Antilles is still subject to the Netherlands. Saint Kitts and Nevis, Antigua, and Montserrat are some of the nations that are still considered subjects of the British Crown.

Some of these Caribbean nations are moving toward a new era. In 2021, the country of Barbados became its own republic, although it still remains part of the British Commonwealth.

Is this a sign of things to come for other nations still subject to European powers? Will we see a new era of Caribbean history written in the 21st century? Only time will tell, but for now, it is important to understand the region's past so we can understand its future.

What This Book Will Cover

In this book, you will learn about the history of the Caribbean, beginning with its earliest years in recorded history. Here is a breakdown of what you will find in each chapter:

- **Chapter 1:** This chapter will cover the early beginnings of the Taíno tribe and the exploration of Christopher Columbus. Columbus's initial discovery led him to establish a foothold in the region in the name of the Spanish Crown, but his voyages turned up next to nothing in his promise to provide Spain with riches.

- **Chapter 2:** Columbus's discovery of the Caribbean set the stage for Spain's dominance over the region. It would enjoy its many claims to the region until it entered battles with England later on in the 17th century. France would eventually join the fray as well. However, the European nations would also find themselves doing battle with an enemy that was beholden to no sovereign nation.

- **Chapter 3:** The European wars of religion would soon reverberate beyond its shores. It pitted one European power against another. Alliances were made, and new tensions were created. The wars of religion would last well over three centuries, with the Caribbean region right in the middle of the fight.

- **Chapter 4:** Colonial laws began to take shape in an effort to regulate plantations in the Caribbean. The slave trade began to grow thanks to the rising number of plantations. Rebellion was not tolerated, which led to serious punishments, including death. In the Caribbean, many Afro-Caribbeans, including slaves and free people, outnumbered their European counterparts. This led to Haiti's rise against France in its fight for independence. The twelve-year war resulted in the victory of the Afro-Caribbeans, making Haiti the second nation in the Americas to defeat a European power and become an independent nation. The 19th century witnessed many rebellions throughout the Caribbean, and the abolition of slavery became a reality.

- **Chapter 5:** The Caribbean was the theater for many wars during the colonial period. The wars covered in this chapter will include the various battles between European powers, the American and French Revolutions, and the Napoleonic Wars.

- **Chapter 6:** At the start of the 20th century, Spain was embroiled in a war with the United States, with its last two interests in the Caribbean on the line. The war resulted in the transfer of power of two of Spain's colonies: Cuba and Puerto Rico. This chapter will also cover the interests the United States had in the Caribbean, which date back to 1823 with President James Monroe's Monroe Doctrine.

- **Chapter 7:** In the 20th century, the Caribbean witnessed an economic decline in one of the region's top commodities: sugar. The Caribbean soon became a tourist destination, with people from different parts of North America visiting during the winter months. This chapter will also cover the Caribbean nations' efforts during the First World War. Meanwhile, the Caribbean's black population would soon fight for more rights in their respective countries.

- **Chapter 8:** Some of the Caribbean nations were ruled under brutal dictatorships. This chapter will cover the regimes of Rafael Trujillo in the Dominican Republic, François "Papa Doc" Duvalier in Haiti, and the regimes of Fulgencio Batista and Fidel Castro of Cuba. Some of the independent Caribbean nations witnessed an exodus of people leaving their home countries for the United States, a place where people believed freedom was possible.

- **Chapter 9:** When Cuba became communist, the Soviet Union saw a chance to spread the ideology throughout the region. This chapter will cover the incident that occurred in Grenada in 1983, which involved the United States and other Caribbean nations.

- **Chapter 10:** After the collapse of the Soviet Union, Cuba still maintained its status as a communist country, but it was no longer the site of a greater threat. Today, the United States still maintains its interests in the Caribbean as a strategic and economic partner. This chapter will cover the relationships between the Caribbean nations and the world's major powers from the late 20th century to the present day.

Throughout these ten chapters, we will unveil the rich history the Caribbean region has witnessed. Explore how the people of the Caribbean fought for political and social change while being ruled by colonial powers. Discover how they witnessed brutality and genocide at the hands of their own people in the mid-20th century. And learn how the Caribbean nations are taking action to become more peaceful and prosperous today.

If you wish to learn more about the captivating history of the Caribbean, all that's left now is to turn to the next page and begin Chapter 1.

Chapter 1 – Early History: Pre-Discovery and the Exploration of Christopher Columbus

The Caribbean's recorded history begins with the discovery of Italian explorer Christopher Columbus. However, before his arrival, a number of tribes already resided in the region.

This chapter will go over what we know about the history of the Caribbean during the pre-discovery years. We will also discuss Christopher Columbus's exploration. His intent was to travel to Asia to prosper from the lucrative spice trade. However, his desire to travel west to find Asia led him to discover a new part of the world, at least to the Europeans.

At the time of his voyage, many nations were looking to expand beyond their borders. They were also looking for goods to sell that they couldn't find in their own country.

Christopher Columbus's discovery of the Caribbean led to a surge in exploration over the next two centuries. But for now, let's take a look at the early history of the Caribbean.

Pre-discovery Years: The Taíno and Other Indigenous Tribes

The first people to land in the present-day Caribbean are believed to have inhabited the region as early as 5000 BCE. The Taíno people are believed to have originated from South America, although it is unclear where exactly they came from before settling on the continent.

The first inhabitants resided on an island named Ayiti ("land of high mountains"). The island was later named Hispaniola after Columbus's discovery; it contains the present-day nations of Haiti and the Dominican Republic.

Little is known about Ayiti between its early settlement and the time of Christopher Columbus's arrival. We do know the Taíno resided on the island, though, due to archaeological excavations.

By the time the 15th century rolled around, the Taíno had expanded across much of the Caribbean. They lived mostly in Haiti, the Dominican Republic, Cuba, Jamaica, and Puerto Rico, although groups of them also lived in Florida.

The Taíno separated into three different groups. The Western Taíno lived in Cuba, The Bahamas, and Jamaica. (As a side note, it is known as The Bahamas with a capital "T" since that is its official name.) The Classic Taíno settled in Puerto Rico and Hispaniola. The Eastern Taíno resided in the Lesser Antilles nations, those closest to South America. A lesser-known Taíno tribe made the trek farther north and landed in parts of Florida.

By the time Columbus made his presence known in 1492, numerous chiefdoms and territories in the Caribbean were already claimed by the Taíno. In Cuba alone, there were nearly thirty chiefdoms. When Columbus claimed Cuba for the Spanish Crown in 1492, many towns and cities were named after Taíno chiefdoms.

The Igneri People

The Igneri people are believed to have inhabited the Windward Islands of the Lesser Antilles. They were a subgroup of the Arawaks, as were the Taíno. The Igneri were wiped out by the Carib tribes that likely came to the Caribbean from South America.

The Caribs mostly lived in South America and the Lesser Antilles, but they did not speak an Arawak language. When the Spanish arrived, they used the term "Arawak" to refer to friendly natives and "Caribs" to refer to hostile ones. "Carib" is similar to the Arawak word for "cannibal," and the Europeans reported on how the Caribs (or Kalinago) ate human flesh.

The Carib men might have coupled with the Igneri women after killing off the men of the tribe. However, this has not been proven, although, over time, the Igneri began speaking Carib, so it might be possible.

The Igneri language originated from the Arawak language of South America. The Taíno language was distinct but had similarities to the Arawak language. Some historians believed the Caribs conquered the Igneri but never banished them from their territories. The Igneri might have been absorbed into the Carib tribe and learned their language. Unfortunately, we don't have solid proof of what actually occurred, so we have to resort to theories.

The Kalinago

The Kalinago were known by a different name: Caribs or Island Caribs. Like the Igneri, they resided in the Lesser Antilles, specifically the Windward Islands. The Caribbean would earn its name from the Carib tribe.

The Caribs originated from South America, heading to the Caribbean sometime around 1200 BCE. The Kalinago are believed to have outlived their Taíno counterparts, although both were devastated by European colonization. Today, there are small pockets of ethnic Caribs that reside in the Lesser Antilles.

The Garifuna

The Garifuna people, or the Black Caribs, lived in the Lesser Antilles and the island today known as Saint Vincent. They originated from Africa, although there is evidence of indigenous American ancestry. The Garifuna are believed to be the first people to bring African influences and culture to the Americas.

Their arrival is believed to be dated back to the early 1300s CE. Their point of origin is West Africa (specifically the Mali Empire). They used their cultural staples, such as dance and music, even in times of struggle, especially when future West Africans became slaves in the colonies. Some historians argue that the Garifuna arrived later, swimming to shore from capsized slave ships sometime in the mid-1600s.

The Macorix

The Macorix tribe is believed to have lived in the area of Hispaniola, the part now known as the Dominican Republic. They spoke a much different language compared to the Taíno, but it is known the Taíno shared Hispaniola with the Macorix people.

Tribes in Florida

Before the discovery of Florida, two indigenous tribes were known to have inhabited the area. The first was the Tequesta, who were situated on the southeastern coast. They were once believed to have been closely related to the Taíno, but there is no definite proof of this yet. It seems unlikely, considering how long the Tequesta lived in Florida.

It was once believed the Lucayans, a branch of the Taíno who settled in The Bahamas, came from Florida due to how close the two territories are. However, it seems unlikely due to the lack of archaeological evidence; the more likely theory is they came from Cuba and Hispaniola. The Lucayans were the first indigenous Americans that Christopher Columbus met.

Christopher Columbus: Before the Voyage

Christopher Columbus began his exploration of the seas as a young boy. It was believed that during his career as a sailor, he made trips to England, Ireland, and northern Europe as part of an armed convoy that carried precious goods. There were claims that Columbus made trips as far north as Iceland in 1477.

He would join his brother Bartholomew later that same year and continue trading on behalf of one of the wealthiest families in Italy: the Centurione family of Genoa. Columbus spent time in Portugal after his return from the seas and remained there until 1485. He married a daughter of a Portuguese nobleman and started a family of his own.

In the early 1480s, Columbus made trips to West Africa, where he conducted trade on a regular basis. During that time, the Portuguese had colonies in present-day Ghana.

Around this time, Columbus started to seek financial support for his greatest voyage yet. His goal was to create a foothold in the lucrative trading routes between Europe and Asia by sailing west. If he was successful, he could bring back spices and silk to Spain and be paid handsomely for his work.

In 1484, he began to request support from King John II of Portugal. The king turned to his advisors to review the proposal, which was ultimately rejected due to issues with the proposed distance. Columbus waited another four years before submitting another unsuccessful proposal.

Columbus looked elsewhere, as he was determined to set out on his voyage and make history. In 1486, he was able to speak with Queen Isabella of Spain, who sent the proposal over to a committee.

The committee believed Columbus had underestimated the distance of the westward route between Spain and Asia. Thus, the proposal was declined, although the Crown retained it for future use. Spain would soon provide Columbus with an annual salary of fourteen thousand maravedis, which was about the yearly pay for a sailor.

The Kingdom of Spain would send him ten thousand more maravedis while providing him free food and lodging. The Spanish wanted to make sure Columbus's idea was not heard by any other nation. In 1489, Columbus sent his brother Bartholomew to England to see if King Henry VII would be willing to sponsor the voyage.

While en route to England, Bartholomew was captured by pirates. He was released but did not reach England until 1491. Meanwhile, Spain sent Columbus another payment to help him pay for supplies and requested his presence to discuss his voyage.

Columbus soon met with Ferdinand and Isabella at Granada in January 1492. The discussions continued until April, but at long last, an agreement was reached. Columbus received his funding, and if his voyage was successful, he would be provided with the rank of "Admiral of the Ocean Sea." He would also be appointed viceroy and governor of any lands he claimed in the name of the Spanish Crown.

Columbus was given the authority to nominate three people for the offices of the lands he claimed, although the monarchs got the final say. In addition, he would receive 10 percent of the revenue that was brought in.

The First Voyage

Columbus began his first voyage on August 3rd, 1492. He had a crew of ninety men and three ships: the famous *Nina*, *Pinta*, and *Santa Maria*. The ships departed from Palos de la Frontera, Spain.

Columbus wanted to reach Asia via a westward route. Back then, most people believed the world was round, so Columbus thought it was possible to reach Asia from the west, discovering new lands for Spain on the way. He was correct that Asia was accessible from the west, but his calculations were incorrect due to his estimation of the Earth's circumference being smaller than it really is.

During the voyage, Columbus and his crew believed they were close to land due to the presence of birds. On October 12th, they landed on one of the islands of The Bahamas known as San Salvador. Columbus was under the assumption he had landed somewhere in the East Indies.

He would spend the remainder of 1492 hopping from one island to another in search of spices, gold, silver, and other precious goods. He wasn't able to find much of these commodities, though. According to his journal entries from August to November of 1492, he documented his discovery of the marine wildlife and the crew's mood. There is some mention of the natives having gold but no mention of Columbus obtaining any for himself. When he left for Spain in 1493, he brought back small amounts of gold to show what precious goods could be found in the Americas.

Columbus also suggested that the Taíno (more specifically, the Lucayans) should be enslaved. He said, "With 50 men they can all be subjugated and made to do what is required of them." Large-scale enslavement didn't happen until Columbus's return voyage in 1493, but he did take hostages and took several Taíno back to Spain. In early 1493, Columbus left Hispaniola, with some members of his crew remaining behind to tend to the settlement they had created.

The Second Voyage: Return to Hispaniola

Six months after returning from his initial voyage, Columbus launched a second voyage. He decided to return to Hispaniola to see what had happened to the settlement. It had been destroyed. It is believed the Europeans had mistreated the nearby indigenous people, who decided they had had enough and massacred the settlers.

Columbus assigned his brothers, Bartholomew and Diego, with the task of rebuilding the settlement. While doing so, the Columbus brothers and some of the crew would enslave hundreds of Taíno. Christopher would soon search farther west to find gold.

His quest for riches turned up nothing. In lieu of the gold that he promised Queen Isabella, Columbus brought her five hundred Taíno. Two hundred of them died on the voyage, and many died after being sold into slavery. The queen did not want the Taíno to be enslaved. In fact, she decreed they should be treated as equal subjects, as she saw them as potential converts to Christianity. However, Columbus and others continued to mistreat the Taíno and other indigenous peoples.

Third and Final Voyage

Columbus sailed back over the Atlantic for the third time in May 1498. This time, he visited Trinidad and parts of South America. He would soon return to Hispaniola, where he found the settlement had once again been destroyed.

Many of the colonists and Taíno had staged a revolution against Bartholomew and Diego Columbus, accusing them of mismanaging the colony and abusing them. The Spanish Crown soon appointed a new governor, but the number of Taíno continued to dwindle.

By the mid-16th century, a quarter million Taíno inhabited the island; it is unknown how many Taíno existed by the time Columbus arrived, with estimates ranging from sixty thousand to eight million.

Misfortune would strike Columbus, as he was stripped of his titles and arrested by Spanish authorities in 1500 due to his brutality (some argue it was because of his aggression against the natives, while others say it was because of his mistreatment of the European colonists). He was released a little over a month later. In May 1502, Columbus's final voyage began. On this voyage, he explored Panama and other parts of Central America.

By the time Columbus's last voyage set out, the sovereigns had little confidence in him, who was in ill health. Ferdinand and Isabella forbade him to return to Hispaniola to avoid a repeat of what had occurred years before. Half of the ships Columbus brought with him were destroyed by storms and the indigenous peoples of the territories he happened upon.

In June 1503, one of Columbus's pilots made a turn to the north. A storm hit the fleet, and they were forced to make landfall in Jamaica, where they were trapped for quite some time. When he had set out, Columbus promised the Spanish Crown that it would be his best voyage yet. However, it was perhaps his unluckiest trip, and he missed his good fortune by the smallest thread, as he missed the opportunity to discover the Pacific Ocean via Panama. He also probably failed to meet the Maya, although it is possible he encountered them when he sailed to the Yucatán Peninsula.

Columbus returned to Spain, where he would die in 1506. His promise to the Spanish Crown was never fulfilled. However, his accidental discovery of a new part of the world inspired Spain and other nations to explore more of the area.

Columbus returned to the Caribbean even after his death. In 1542, Columbus's son Diego had his father's remains interred as his dying wish. The pair were entombed at the cathedral in Santo Domingo in the Dominican Republic. However, according to some accounts, the remains were exhumed after Hispaniola was transferred to the French and reinterred in Cuba. And then, supposedly, his remains were moved after the Spanish-American War to Seville, Spain.

There are claims that some of Columbus's bones may still be interred in the Caribbean. A memorial known as the Columbus Lighthouse was erected; it is located in Santo Domingo, Dominican Republic.

Final Thoughts

The Taíno were among the first people to set foot in the Caribbean. We still do not know much about their early presence, but the further discovery of artifacts and tribal markings will help scholars come to more conclusions. Regardless, they made contact with Columbus and the Spaniards, which changed their society forever.

The number of Taíno was soon reduced. Many became slaves, and the large presence of Taíno would be cut down to thousands instead of millions. The Taíno were once declared extinct, but recent DNA evidence shows there are many living descendants of the Taíno in the Caribbean.

Christopher Columbus failed to capitalize on the opportunity of the Asian spice trade. He did his best to make up for this by discovering new precious items for his sovereign benefactors.

To his credit, the discovery of the Caribbean gave Spain an opportunity to expand its territory beyond Europe. Word of his discovery also drew the attention of much of Europe. Soon, Spain would discover that it was not the only nation with vested interests in the New World.

Chapter 2 – Post-Columbus Era and the Rise of European Nations

Spain and other European nations soon capitalized on Columbus's accidental discovery. They were now aware the opportunity for new colonies existed. The potential of finding riches was still great, despite Columbus's inability to produce what he said he could.

When Columbus discovered the Caribbean and parts of the Americas, much of Europe took note. Nations like the Netherlands, France, and England would soon have their own interests in the region. Yet, the two nations of the Iberian Peninsula—Portugal and Spain—kicked things off by snatching up lands in South and Central America. They brought gold back to their home countries, bolstering their wealth.

The success of the two nations piqued the interests of the other European powers. Most of these nations would wait nearly a century or more before voyaging to the New World, though.

This chapter will go over the history of the colonies established by Spain and Portugal. Although these colonies sent home riches, they were not without problems. The European nations would have to contend with the pirates who trolled the high seas in search of ships to rob.

In the post-Columbus Caribbean, intense battles were fought for the highest stakes imaginable.

Spain Asserts Its Dominance

After Columbus's death, Spain picked up where the explorer left off. Spain had no plans to conquer the leftover members of the Taíno. But when many Spaniards arrived in the region, the Taíno attempted to resist their advances.

The Spanish continued to discover the Caribbean and Central and South America over the course of the 1500s. Columbus's claim that parts of Central America had spices and gold was eventually proven true.

Spanish colonists soon found themselves settling in areas where many indigenous peoples resided. The native people were agriculturalists and ruled by their own tribal leaders. The Spaniards took advantage of their manpower and used them for the extraction of materials and other precious goods, which they sent home.

The remaining Taíno were enslaved under the authority of Spanish conquistadors. While indigenous slavery was outlawed in Spain, Ferdinand and Isabella approved it in their colonies. The Taínos' major challenges were diseases, starvation, and brutality, which greatly reduced their numbers.

Foreign diseases were likely the number one killer of indigenous peoples. These silent killers would not affect the Europeans, who had brought them to the New World to begin with. The Europeans had built-up immunity to diseases like smallpox, while the natives had none.

The deaths of so many natives threatened Spain's prospects of extracting materials since they relied on slaves to make up for lost numbers. The Spanish were able to acquire slaves from other parts of the Caribbean, including Jamaica, Cuba, and Puerto Rico.

Slavery had already existed in the Caribbean prior to the Europeans' arrival. Warring tribes would take prisoners of war as slaves. Their intent was to have the slaves work to create tribute for the chief who had imprisoned them.

This kind of slavery functioned under a kinship system. This was similar to the practices that were done in Central and West Africa before the transatlantic slave trade began.

Establishment of the Law of Burgos

In 1511, a Dominican clergyman named Antonio de Montesinos used a sermon to call out Spain's cruelty and abuse of slaves.

These abuses were also noticed in the writing of another clergyman named Bartolomé de las Casas. Nearly thirty years after Montesinos's sermon, de las Casas wrote what was known as the Black Legend. The writings contained anti-Spanish sentiments.

The sermon caused unrest among many settlers of Hispaniola. Yet, it empowered Casas to galvanize his mission against Spain's cruelty toward the Taíno. This resulted in the Crown establishing the Law of Burgos, which was designed to protect the indigenous peoples by regulating their treatment.

The Law of Burgos was restricted to Hispaniola initially but later applied to some of the other Caribbean islands claimed by Spain, including Puerto Rico and Jamaica (which was then named Santiago).

The law also put labor regulations in place, such as how the workers were treated. Women who were more than four months pregnant were exempt from any kind of heavy labor. The laws took effect on December 27th, 1512.

The Explorations of Ponce de Léon

One of the first explorers to do the bidding of the Spanish Crown was Juan Ponce de Léon.

In 1508, Ponce de Léon and his crew arrived in Puerto Rico. The island nation would soon be under Spanish control. The capital of San Juan began construction in 1511 and was officially established a decade later. San Juan has since been the capital of Puerto Rico.

Puerto Rico was under the dominion of Spain for over four hundred years. Spanish control began when Columbus landed in 1493 and was not relinquished until 1898, near the end of the Spanish-American War.

In regards to Puerto Rico's early settlement, Ponce de Léon was the governor of the island from 1508 to 1519, with a sizable gap between 1511 and 1515.

For de Léon's exploration efforts in the New World, the Spanish royals knighted him upon his return to Spain in 1514. King Ferdinand reinstated him as governor of Puerto Rico and also gave him the authority to return to Florida and create a colony there. Two years later, death came for Ferdinand, and the plans for a settlement in Florida were delayed for a few years.

As part of being knighted, Ponce de Léon was awarded his own coat of arms. He was the first Spanish explorer to be given this honor, which he received for his successful exploration and creation of Spanish colonies in the Caribbean.

During his time in Spain, the Spanish Crown drew up a new contract. It provided Ponce de Léon the right to settle and govern Florida and a chain of islands in The Bahamas known as Bimini. The Spanish Crown assumed that Florida was an island; it did not know that it was part of the North American mainland. The contract also included the usual terms for sharing gold and other precious goods with the Crown.

To fight off Caribs and other invaders, the Spanish Crown ordered Ponce de Léon to form an armada that could subdue any threat. Spanish settlements were under continuous attack from the Caribs, and something needed to be done to secure their safety. Armed with his ships, Ponce de Léon departed Spain on May 14th, 1515.

After departing Spain, it is believed Ponce de Léon and his small armada encountered Caribs near Guadeloupe, although there may have been a couple of other skirmishes in the area as well. When King Ferdinand died in 1516, Ponce de Léon made his return to Spain to preserve the titles and privileges that had been given to him by the late sovereign.

Ponce de Léon would remain in Spain for another two years before he finally returned to Puerto Rico. In 1521, he began planning for what would be his final voyage to Florida. He organized a crew of two hundred men and brought along various livestock and farming equipment.

Ponce de Léon arrived in an area believed to be southwest Florida near present-day Charlotte Harbor. His crew was soon confronted by the Calusa tribe that resided in the area. In the ensuing skirmish, Ponce de Léon was injured.

The crew left Florida and found refuge in Havana. However, Ponce de Léon's injuries were too severe, resulting in his death. It is believed that he was struck by a poisoned arrow.

His remains were returned to Puerto Rico, where he was interred in the San José Church. In 1836, his remains were exhumed and reinterred at the Cathedral of San Juan Bautista in Puerto Rico.

Diego Columbus: Continuing the Family Legacy

Two years after the death of Christopher Columbus, his son Diego was named the governor of the Indies. He made his home in Santo Domingo the following year, 1509. For one of his major acts, he sent Diego Velázquez de Cuellar to acquire neighboring Cuba.

By 1511, Cuba, Hispaniola, Cuba, Puerto Rico, and Jamaica were under Diego Columbus's authority. As part of his role as governor, he was entitled to a tenth of Spain's income. Due to his increase in wealth and power, Diego and many of King Ferdinand's officials began to clash, forming factions against each other.

The king recalled Diego back to Spain in 1514. Although Diego had to wait five long years, his powers were restored by Charles V, Emperor of the Holy Roman Empire and King of Spain. Diego finally returned to Santo Domingo on November 12th, 1520.

Upon his return, Diego witnessed a revolt that was taking place near the Franciscan missions along the Cumana River. After failed attempts to settle the area and due to Diego's friction with those in charge, Charles recalled Diego back to Spain in 1523.

In the early 1520s, the first rebellion of slaves in the Americas took place. The rebellion was started in Santo Domingo by slaves who were working on a sugar plantation owned by Diego. Many of the slaves fled the area and found refuge amongst the remaining members of the Taíno. However, some of the rebelling slaves were arrested and executed.

Diego Columbus would live out his remaining years in Spain, where he died on February 23rd, 1526. His son, Luis, was appointed admiral of the Indies.

French Exploration of the Caribbean

By the mid-16th century, France had already achieved success in exploration. The French wished to spread the Catholic religion throughout parts of the New World. Their first major exploration began in 1534 when Jacques Cartier arrived in present-day Canada and claimed the land around the St. Lawrence River on behalf of the French Crown.

Cartier claimed there were riches in the area, but these claims turned out to be exaggerations, as France saw a low yield on its returns. Cartier was unable to establish a successful colony.

France had a small presence in the area near present-day Jacksonville, Florida, with Fort Caroline. In 1565, Spanish forces from St. Augustine drove out the French and destroyed the fort in the process. Thus, the stage for war between the two countries was set.

Samuel de Champlain, who would become a successful explorer in his own right, made trips to the Caribbean after the war between France and Spain had ended. In the beginning, Champlain and his uncle, Captain Provencal, were tasked by King Henry IV to return captured Spanish soldiers to their home country.

Once the soldiers made it back to Spanish soil, the Frenchmen didn't return home. Instead, they were tasked to voyage to the Caribbean. Champlain made three separate trips between 1599 to 1601 to Spanish colonies in the Americas, including the Virgin Islands and Puerto Rico.

He reported his findings to Henry IV, which included his discovery of the plants and animals of the region. He also sent the king maps of the region, which would prove useful to many explorers in the subsequent years.

Champlain is believed to be one of the first people to suggest the creation of the Panama Canal. However, he would never see that project come to fruition in his lifetime; the canal would eventually be created more than three hundred years later. Although Champlain had been exploring on behalf of Spain, his findings set the stage for France to colonize parts of the Caribbean.

Over the next few years, Champlain made his way north to establish colonies on behalf of France in parts of present-day Canada. France would not establish a permanent colony in the Caribbean until 1625.

France was intent on establishing its dominance in the trade market. The French mainly wanted to trade coffee and sugar. They had slaves imported from Africa to work the plantations. Saint-Domingue was the site of one of France's (and the world's) richest colonies.

Although Saint-Domingue (modern-day Haiti) was incredibly successful, it didn't start off that way. French buccaneers created a settlement there in 1625, but the Spanish were resistant to their presence, burning down their settlements time and time again.

Thus, Saint-Domingue was not France's first permanent colony in the Caribbean. That honor belongs to Saint Kitts, with the colony being established in 1627 (some sources say 1625). By that time, the English had already established a colony of their own there. The French and English divided the island, although tensions constantly rose between the two parties. The island was tugged back and forth between the two nations until the British established themselves as the winners in 1783.

Pierre Belain d'Esnambuc, a trader and explorer, discovered Saint Kitts for the French. He also created a French settlement on Martinique and Guadeloupe in 1635.

The colony on Martinique, Saint-Pierre, used the land for sugarcane production. The French on the island were involved in several battles with the Caribs. It got to the point where the colonists had to move to the eastern side of the island.

After Belain's death in 1636, his nephew, Jacques Dyel du Parquet, took over the colony. He was appointed governor of Martinique in 1636 and remained on the island. Soon afterward, Fort Saint Louis was built; this fort would eventually be destroyed and rebuilt as Fort-Royal (today, it is known as Fort-de-France).

Du Parquet expanded France's presence in the Caribbean. He decided that France's best chances were in the south. In 1643, the French established a permanent settlement on Saint Lucia, and in 1649, the French settled the island nation of Grenada.

In the early 1640s, Compagnie des Îles de l'Amérique ("Company of the American Islands") renewed its charter for the next twenty years. However, the company didn't survive to see the next twenty years, as it was dissolved in 1651. Throughout its lifespan (1635–1651), the company had claims to Guadeloupe, Martinique, Saint Lucia, Saint Martin, Grenada, Saint Barts, and Saint Croix.

After the company's dissolution, the du Parquet family purchased the islands of Martinique, Saint Lucia, and Grenada. Charles d'Houël du Petit Pré, who was the governor of Guadeloupe at the time, purchased the island he oversaw, along with three small islands nearby.

The Knights of Malta, led by Philippe de Longvilliers de Poincy, purchased Saint Croix, Saint Martin, Saint Kitts, and Saint Barts.

Dutch Arrival in the Caribbean

Charles I of Spain (better remembered as Charles V, Emperor of the Holy Roman Empire) inherited the Netherlands before being crowned Holy Roman emperor in 1519.

In time, the Netherlands became one of the largest economic and military powers in the world. By this point, its government was more of a republic, not an absolute monarchy. This was a contrast to when it was under Habsburg rule from 1482 to 1581.

The people of the Netherlands did their part to help their country and were rewarded for their efforts. The merchants paid taxes to the government, allowing the country to become wealthy. In return, the Netherlands was able to defend its borders against intruders while taking care of its people and expanding.

The Dutch focused on religious expansion. Unlike France and Spain, which were both Catholic nations, the Netherlands was heavily Protestant. The Dutch were intent on spreading Calvinism and willing to explore the New World to spread their message.

In 1602, the Dutch East India Company was established to carry out trade in Asia. In 1621, the Dutch West India Company was formed, creating a foothold for trade in the Americas, which included the Caribbean. The Dutch had already laid claim to territories in North America, such as parts of present-day New York, including New York City. However, they were not yet established in the Caribbean.

That wouldn't be the case for long. The Dutch made their first settlement in the Caribbean in 1628. Although they built a fort on the modern-day island of Tobago, indigenous tribes attacked the settlement. The Dutch abandoned it for three years but came back in 1633 to reestablish it. This time around, the Spanish would destroy it, doing so in retaliation for the Netherlands' support of a revolt on the neighboring island of Trinidad.

Tobago saw attempts at colonization by several European countries. Aside from the Netherlands, England, France, Spain, and even Sweden had interests in the island. Tobago changed hands thirty-three times before it was finally handed over to Great Britain in 1814 as part of the Treaty of Paris.

The Dutch also settled on the islands of Bonaire and Curaçao in the southern Caribbean in 1634. Within the next six years, they made claims on other islands, such as Sint Eustatius (Dutch for Saint Eustatius) in 1636 and Aruba in 1637.

Around 1640, the Dutch claimed smaller islands, namely Tortola, Virgin Gorda, Jost van Dyke, and Saba. Needless to say, the Dutch made themselves known in the Caribbean.

England's Claims in the Caribbean

England's presence in the Caribbean was part of its grand expansion throughout the world. It was intent on establishing a shorter route to Asia and believed the answer to its problem lay in the west. English sailors were highly skilled and proficient, especially when it came to long voyages.

One of the first Englishman to make his way to the Caribbean was John Hawkins, who traveled there in the 1560s. He was able to transport many slaves from Africa to sell to the Spanish throughout their many colonies in the west. Hawkins found success, but the work he did was considered illegal.

However, some of the Spanish authorities thought nothing of it and paid Hawkins for his services. The Spanish government eventually learned of these actions and protested that a Catholic nation had no business making trades with a Protestant nation like England. Hawkins's next voyages were not as successful.

Despite being the chief architect for the Royal Navy, John Hawkins is not as well known as English privateer Francis Drake, who headed a mission to Panama in the 1570s. It was not his first time sailing in the Caribbean, though; he actually worked under John Hawkins. Drake was the first Englishman to see the Pacific

Ocean, and he would later circumnavigate the globe.

But in the 1570s, his goal wasn't circumnavigation; his focus was on attacking Spanish settlements. Drake's biggest score would come in March 1573 when he captured Nombre de Dios, which was known for its reserves of silver.

As a result of Drake's attack and seizure of Spanish ships and settlements, the relations between England and Spain took a downward turn. When Drake captured Nombre de Dios, the two countries were at peace, although tensions were already on the rise. By 1585, the Spanish had made it their mission to capture English ships. The Anglo-Spanish War, which began in 1585, would last until 1604.

Drake made an appearance in 1588 in the southern Caribbean while en route to South America. He was confronted with a Spanish armada, which he and his crew were able to successfully beat back. This served to prove that England was a power on the rise.

Meanwhile, another English sailor named Walter Raleigh sought to establish a colony in the Americas. He took up residence in Trinidad in 1595, pushing the Spanish out. He explored the Caribbean in search of the mysterious city of gold known as El Dorado.

Raleigh did not find the fabled city, although he was fairly successful at repelling the Spanish and earning the natives' trust. He went back to England with not much to show for his efforts. Eventually, his relations with King James I soured, and Raleigh was executed in 1618.

By the time the English had turned their attention to the Caribbean, they had already established a successful settlement in the Americas. In 1607, they established Jamestown in present-day Virginia. Its success was due to its tobacco crops.

However, the English saw the Caribbean as an opportunity to expand on their already successful tobacco economy. One of the first islands the English settled was Bermuda. The ships landed there due to a storm in 1609. By 1612, they had created Bermuda's capital, St. George. Hamilton became Bermuda's capital in 1815.

Bermuda is often included in the list of Caribbean nations, but Bermuda is actually north of the Caribbean Sea. The first successful

English settlement in the Caribbean was established in 1623 when the island of Saint Kitts was claimed on behalf of the English Crown. The English soon met with interference from the French, who established their own colony on the island. As we talked about above, the two split the island; however, peace wasn't in the cards for them. The British expelled their French counterparts in the late 1700s.

The English established settlements on Barbados in 1627 and Nevis, an island near Saint Kitts, in 1628. These islands were perfect for planting and growing tobacco.

Sadly, the settlers on these islands fell ill due to various diseases, such as cholera, typhus, and influenza, among others. These diseases had been prevalent since Columbus's discovery of the Caribbean. Aside from settlers, indigenous tribes were hardest hit due to their unfamiliarity with such diseases and the lack of care (compared to what the colonists were receiving).

Because of the dwindling numbers, the English relied on indentured servants from their own nation to keep the settlements afloat. However, with the overproduction of tobacco in the Caribbean and Virginia, its price would tumble.

England decided to diversify its crops rather than rely on only one, even if that one crop was in high demand. So, the English started to grow cotton and maize. Their attempts to cash in on these crops were not as fruitful, although cotton would make up nearly half of Britain's exports in the late 1700s.

The English would soon get their foot in the door of the sugar trade. Sugar crops brought prosperity to the Caribbean region for several centuries. In 1632, England established the islands of Antigua and Montserrat (the latter was settled by Irish Catholics). England wouldn't establish another settlement for nearly two decades, adding Anguilla in 1650 and finally Tortola in 1672.

England also notably laid claim to Jamaica in 1655. The previous year, Oliver Cromwell planned a surprise attack on the Spanish, who possessed the island at the time. His intent was to strengthen England's economy while finding a place for veterans of the Wars of the Three Kingdoms (related conflicts that took place in England, Ireland, and Scotland) to settle because of their discontent with England.

Cromwell also took it upon himself to declare war on Spain. This was due to the fact that he did not approve of Catholicism. The Puritans in England were considered the religious authority at the time.

A fleet left England with nearly three thousand crew members, including sailors and troops. They soon met with other English forces in the West Indies, with their numbers amounting to nearly eight thousand. General Robert Venables and Admiral William Penn shared command.

Spain realized England's intent to invade the Caribbean months before the English fleet's departure. The Spanish correctly assumed England was going to target Hispaniola, so they beefed up their defenses around the island.

In January 1655, the English arrived in Barbados, where they remained for a couple of months. On April 13th, Venables's forces arrived in Santo Domingo (the Dominican Republic). Four thousand men were ready to take arms upon their arrival; more than one thousand of them died due to combat or illness.

Venables and his men left Santo Domingo on April 25th. Venables and Penn had not been on friendly terms during the voyage. And Venables's loss in Santo Domingo further deteriorated their relationship.

The men believed Jamaica, being a smaller island, would mean less resistance. With their original mission of capturing Santo Domingo a failure, Penn and Venables found an alternative opportunity. It would soon become one that decided the fates of both men.

Penn took his fleet to Jamaica, where they were spotted on May 19th by Spanish settlers. Two days later, Penn and his crew arrived in Caguaya Bay. The Spanish forces defending the area soon surrendered.

An ill Venables made his way to Santiago de la Vega, which had been claimed by Penn after his attack on the Spanish, nearly a week later. He made the terms of England's claim clear. Jamaica was now under England's authority. The English gave the Spanish settlers a chance to leave the island or face death; many of them fled to Cuba.

Penn headed home in June 1655. Venables would arrive about two months later, still sick and malnourished. Because of their failure to capture Hispaniola, Cromwell punished both Penn and Venables by imprisoning them in the Tower of London.

Soon after, Penn and Venables were released. Penn rebuilt his life as a politician. His son, also known as William Penn, would become an explorer in his own right, establishing what is known as present-day Pennsylvania.

For Venables, his military career came to an end, although he was appointed to serve as governor of Chester. But he was removed from the position when Charles II was restored to the throne.

Venables became a supporter of Nonconformists, a religious group that refused to conform with the Church of England and its governance. His remaining years were mostly quiet, and he died on December 10th, 1687.

Piracy in the Caribbean

"In an honest service there is thin commons, low wages, and hard labour. In this, plenty and satiety, pleasure and ease, liberty and power; and who would not balance creditor on this side, when all the hazard that is run for it, at worst is only a sour look or two at choking. No, a merry life and a short one, shall be my motto." - *"Black Bart" Roberts*

As early as the 16th century, pirates were making their presence known in the Caribbean. The first pirates were experienced in navigation and sea warfare. They sought to capture European ships and steal everything of value from them.

Some pirates had previously been indentured servants in the Caribbean. Henry Morgan might possibly fall under this category, although some think he might have been part of Venables's crew in the attempt to take Hispaniola. Morgan became a privateer (a legal pirate); however, the term "pirate" might fit him better due to his disregard for the legality of attacks. He eventually earned enough money to own a plantation that was worked by slaves. Morgan and his crew became a source of trouble for the Spanish around Jamaica, sailing as far as Venezuela and Panama.

In the beginning, the privateers' targets were ships from other European nations; for instance, English privateers primarily focused on Spanish ships. Piracy was never given full legal status by the colonies, but privateers had their country's blessing. They sailed their own ships and attacked boats of warring nations. They would receive a large share of the spoils, and the Crown would have one less ship to fight on the high seas. They essentially were attacking others as an act of war. Pirates, on the other hand, didn't care about where the ship came from; they were focused more on obtaining treasure than fighting a war.

The English were not the only ones who hired privateers. Before Queen Elizabeth promoted piracy through the use of privateers, France was already giving its men leeway when it came to the Spanish, as King Francis I wanted to weaken both Spain's and Portugal's trade economies. For nearly four decades, privateers from France targeted Spanish ships. Later, privateers from England and the Netherlands performed their own attacks against enemy nations. Although privateers were fighting as part of a war, they knew the Caribbean was filled to the brim with wealth. It made perfect sense to them that they should go where the money was.

Pirates and privateers saw the large number of islands and bays as perfect spots to hide out between plundering targets. They may have been aware the islands often did not have many inhabitants. Many indigenous peoples had been killed by this point, mainly because of diseases, although enslavement and conflicts took a toll as well.

Pirates did not expect too much resistance when they visited an island. Crew members could normally fend off any invaders, and in larger settlements, pirates were able to sell the goods they stole for a price.

France and England often recruited pirates to work as privateers to attack Spanish ships. They would issue letters of marque and give them full confidence in their services. Both France and England also promised not to punish them for piracy (which, at the time, was punishable by execution).

In the 1560s, Spain created a convoy system that would protect its treasure ships from pirate attacks. One route Spain used started in Central America and passed through the Yucatán Channel. The ships used the westerly winds for the latter part of their journey to Europe.

Spain found itself only trading with merchants in its own claims in the Americas, as the Spanish were unable to enforce the trading laws they enacted or control a large area of the seas. This created a hotbed for smuggling and opened up opportunities for other European powers to stake their claims in the Caribbean.

Although Spain attempted to preserve its trade and wealth, its military power diminished. As a result, other nations began to violate trading laws. Piracy continued well into the 1600s, reaching a "golden age" in the 1650s.

In 1651, England passed the Navigation Act. Prior to its creation, England was in the midst of a civil war. Supply lines between North American colonies to England were being disrupted.

England had to improve its trade relations with both the Netherlands and France to keep importing its manufactured goods to its colonies in the Americas. The Navigation Act intended to only allow English ships to import goods to English colonies. Meanwhile, North American colonies were only allowed to export their commodities, such as sugar and tobacco, to England.

It was believed the Navigation Act had provisions that specifically targeted the Dutch. At the time, the Dutch appeared to have considerable control over trade in Europe, and the act excluded the Dutch from directly trading with England.

The two powers would engage in war on three different occasions over the next quarter century. This happened in conjunction with several other wars going on between European countries.

Pirates used this opportunity to do what they did best. The governors of the colonial islands often used pirates to protect their respective claims or fight on behalf of the country as a whole. However, they were unable to control the pirates because of their greed and lack of discipline. And once a war was over, it was very easy for a privateer to slip into piracy.

The European nations eventually stopped relying on pirates and privateers in their wars. They had enough military power to fight on their own. This threatened the livelihood of pirates, especially when the European nations decided to crack down on piracy. The 1717 Transportation Act is one of the first-known policies to combat and punish piracy in the Americas. There was a considerable lack of pirates in the Caribbean by 1720.

Great Britain, which was a superpower by that point, was able to chase off many pirates, especially those near Jamaica. Letters of marque were soon very difficult to get. The Thirty Years' War accelerated the decline of piracy in the Caribbean. However, there was pirate activity well into the 18th century. And although the pirates were suppressed, plenty of smuggling occurred due to the trade laws enacted by the British and Spanish governments.

There are still pirates in the Caribbean today, although their numbers are nowhere near what they were during the Golden Age of Piracy.

Final Thoughts

The post-Columbus era in the Caribbean witnessed years of growth and prosperity. However, many European nations wanted a piece of the region. Wars began to brew, and pirates and privateers began to capitalize on opportunities to live their dream life.

For the next three centuries, the Caribbean served as the backdrop of countless wars between European nations. The wars were fought over more than just land and trade. They also fought to combat different Christian ideologies.

Chapter 3 – The European Wars of Religion and Their Effect on the Caribbean

The four major European nations—Spain, France, England (forming the United Kingdom of Great Britain in 1707), and the Netherlands—each staked their claims in the Caribbean. The nations would battle with each other over trade and territory, but there was an even greater war going on in Europe.

Spain, France, and the Holy Roman Empire were three European nations that were Catholic. Meanwhile, England and the Netherlands were mostly Protestant. Yet, it didn't matter much since two of the Catholic nations squared off against each other in 1635.

While the wars of religion originated in mainland Europe, they would reach the Caribbean. The European nations used the opportunities of exploring the New World to spread their respective religious ideologies. Spain wanted most of the Caribbean natives to convert to Catholicism. However, the Dutch intended to spread Calvinism throughout their claims in the region.

The European wars of religion would last for around two centuries, from the 16th to the early 18th centuries. One of the major wars in this religious conflict was the Thirty Years' War, which was fought because of religious reasons and rivalries between European nations.

How did this war affect the Caribbean, though? Whatever happened in mainland Europe reached the lands that were claimed by the various powers.

The Beginning of the European Wars of Religion

In 1517, a German priest named Martin Luther wrote a letter to Bishop Albrecht von Brandenburg regarding the Catholic Church's sale of indulgences (payment to the church for the forgiveness of sins). The church intended to use the proceeds of the sales to rebuild St. Peter's Basilica.

In the letter, Luther protested the sale and included a copy of his writings entitled "Disputation on the Power and Efficacy of Indulgences." They are also known as the *Ninety-five Theses*. It is believed that on the same day the letter was written, Luther nailed the *Ninety-five Theses* to the door of Castle Church in Wittenberg, Germany. This event kicked off the Reformation.

The copy Albrecht received was sent to Rome so it could be inspected for heretical statements. In June 1520, the pope sent Luther a papal bull (an edict of the church), threatening excommunication from the church unless Luther recanted the *Ninety-five Theses* and forty-one sentences from his previous writings.

Luther burned the papal bull and was excommunicated by the church in January 1521. This led to a schism in the Catholic Church, as those who believed in Luther's writings (which went beyond just condemning the church for the sale of indulgences) broke off and formed Protestant religions. For instance, Lutheranism started on that fateful day in Wittenberg, although many contend that Luther did not set out to separate from the church. His message attracted many followers, especially those from Germany.

Luther would go after the Catholic Church's control over various things, including the doctrine and morality standards. He also used a three-pronged formula: "by faith alone," "by scripture alone," and "by grace alone."

Faith alone or *sola fide* is the belief that a person can be saved by faith alone. Luther believed that no one could earn salvation just by good works.

Scripture alone or *sola scriptura* means that the truth is in the word of God and in the scripture itself. Luther stated the Bible was the authority and a means of communication between God and his people.

Grace alone or *sola gratia* states that a person cannot know the truth about salvation or do good without God's grace. These messages angered many Catholics throughout Europe.

The first violent conflict related to the wars of religion began in 1524 with the German Peasants' War. Luther's teachings and religious and social tensions mixed together, leading to the outbreak of violence.

In the meantime, another clergyman was leading the Reformation. John Calvin believed that God's laws were to be followed and not questioned. He created Calvinism, which soon became predominant in Germany and northern Europe, including the Netherlands. It also made its way into France, leading to the creation of the Huguenots.

The Catholic Church began to challenge Luther's and Calvin's teachings. The Jesuits, an order of the Catholic Church, intended to use education and other means to fend off Protestant heresy.

The wars of religion led to many violent conflicts between 1560 and 1712. In that time period, Europe saw a grand total of thirty years of peace. One of the greatest wars of religion would last just as long and run concurrently with another war that lasted nearly three times as long.

The Eighty Years' War

The Eighty Years' War began in 1568 and ended in 1648. The war pitted the Netherlands and Spain against each other, as the Dutch wanted independence from Spain.

While the war was fought over independence, it was also fought over religion. The Dutch were Protestant, while the Spanish were Catholic. The people of the Netherlands and their territories in the Caribbean were not happy with the rule of the Spanish Habsburgs and their attempts to enforce Catholicism. The Dutch did not face off against the Spanish alone; they got help from the English and the French Huguenots.

At the start of the 17th century, the Spanish and Dutch would often battle each other in the Caribbean. Spain still held the lion's share of the region, while the Dutch were looking to make inroads there to spread Calvinism and galvanize their already booming economy.

The wars of religion weakened Spain's grip on the Caribbean and left many European nations in bad shape on the mainland. This gave England and the Netherlands the opportunity to pick apart the Spanish colonies, beginning with Saint Kitts, Antigua, Nevis, Montserrat, and Bermuda, among others.

Meanwhile, the French managed to make gains in Guadeloupe, Martinique, and the western part of Hispaniola. The Dutch made gains in the southern Caribbean with the annexation of Sint Eustatius and Curaçao.

By the end of the war, Spain recognized Dutch independence (although not all of the Netherlands broke away from Spain at this time).

The Thirty Years' War

The Thirty Years' War began in 1618 and ended alongside the Eighty Years' War in 1648. The Thirty Years' War involved many European nations, both Catholic and Protestant. Toward the end of the war, the conflict became more about who would take over the majority of Europe (and the claims abroad) and less about the religious ideologies that had helped kick off the war in the first place.

Ferdinand II became the Holy Roman emperor in 1619. His first action was to enforce Roman Catholicism on his people. However, religious freedom had been granted to the people in accordance with the Peace of Augsburg, which had been enacted in 1555. This allowed princes in their own realms to adopt either Lutheranism or Catholicism. Citizens of the realm who did not conform to the state religion were free to leave.

The Holy Roman Empire had many semi-autonomous states. By this point, the empire covered all of present-day Germany, Switzerland, and Belgium. It also claimed lands in most of northern

Italy and Austria, among other present-day nations in central Europe.

After the Peace of Augsburg was enacted, the Habsburg kings who ruled Bohemia allowed their Protestant subjects to practice their own religion instead of forcing them to become Catholics. When Rudolf II became king of Bohemia in 1575, he gave Protestants more rights to practice their faith.

When Matthias took over Bohemia in 1611, he continued to grant more religious rights to Protestants, including those residing in his other territories, such as present-day Austria and Hungary.

Ferdinand II, who became king of Bohemia in 1617, wanted to restore what he believed were the "glory days" of the Catholic empire. His interests in Bohemia mostly lay in the resources that were found there.

Ferdinand II claimed that he would honor Rudolf's decrees, but he did not. To make matters worse for the Protestants, Ferdinand granted more lands to the Catholic Church. The lands were originally slated to be used by the Lutherans to build two new churches.

When the Lutherans denounced the action, many of them were arrested by deputy governors. They believed their rights to practice their religion had been infringed. Other Lutherans demanded the prisoners' release, but their pleas were ineffective.

In response, Protestant leaders planned a mass demonstration in Prague on May 23rd, 1618. The demonstration would end up becoming what is known as the 1618 Defenestration of Prague. Protestants descended on Prague Castle, where they met with four lord regents of the Catholic Church.

The Protestants questioned the regents, asking if the latter were responsible for playing a role in Ferdinand II's decision to give the lands to the Catholic Church. The regents asked the Protestants to give them time to meet with their superior authority.

This response did not satisfy the Protestants, as they sought an immediate answer. Two of the regents were spared by the Protestants. But the other two admitted to playing a role in persuading Ferdinand II to hand over the lands to the Catholic Church.

The two and their secretary were thrown out the window. Despite falling seventy feet, all three survived. The Defenestration of Prague resulted in the Catholic Habsburgs and the Protestants preparing for a war that, unbeknownst to them, would last for decades.

Matthias died on March 20th, 1619, with Ferdinand II succeeding him as Holy Roman emperor. Bohemia refused to recognize Ferdinand as its king, so he was replaced by Frederick V, a Protestant. The Bohemian nobles aligned themselves with the Protestant Union, which consisted of several German states that were predominantly Protestant.

In 1635, France joined the Thirty Years' War. Despite being a Catholic nation, the French chose to side with the Protestants to battle their rival, the Habsburgs. Their motives were mostly political rather than religious.

When Ferdinand II died in 1637, his son, Ferdinand III, took over as the Holy Roman emperor and went after France. France ended up in multiple conflicts, fighting the Protestants of France, Spain, and the Holy Roman Empire.

In the 1640s, Portugal began its own revolt against Spain with the help of the Holy Roman Empire. Sweden renewed its conflict with the Habsburgs, which had taken place years before. Denmark-Norway soon found itself fighting alongside the Holy Roman Empire. As you can see, Europe was at war with itself.

The Treaty of Westphalia

The Treaty of Westphalia was signed in 1648, marking the end of both the Eighty Years' War and the Thirty Years' War. The treaty granted independence to the Netherlands and control over its claims in the Caribbean, further weakening Spain's grip on the region.

The treaty allowed the respective nations to be responsible for their own claims, overseeing laws, taxes, and control over the population. This meant that in the Caribbean, the religion that was predominant in the authoritative state was the religion of the land. This meant Curaçao would adhere to Protestantism, while French claims, such as Guadeloupe, were Catholic.

Final Thoughts

The European wars of religion mostly occurred on the European mainland, although the effects of the battles reached well beyond its shores. There is no doubt that battles between some of the warring nations took place in the Caribbean.

The wars of religion affected the way European nations controlled the Caribbean. Spain's dominance would no longer be as strong as it once was, and other European nations would take advantage of that.

Religious freedom was at stake in Europe, which also meant it threatened the Caribbean. But the Treaty of Westphalia would see to it that the European powers established their religion in their own domains.

Chapter 4 – Colonial Laws in the Caribbean

Slavery in the Caribbean existed soon after the Europeans discovered it and lasted for centuries. Many European colonies in the Caribbean and elsewhere relied on the slave trade. Although the Spanish initially used the natives as a source of slave labor, over time, many slaves were imported from Africa. About five million Africans were taken to the Caribbean, where they toiled in the heat and were subjected to harsh conditions. The laws enacted by European powers were used to cement their authority over the slaves.

Slave laws were oppressive. In some colonies, the slaves outnumbered their masters, which made the Europeans fearful of a rebellion.

The laws deterred anyone from rising up and rebelling. The ultimate punishment was execution. However, the time would come when one slave rebellion would become successful and lead to the independence of a nation.

Code Noir: The French Colonial Slave Laws

In 1685, King Louis XIV issued a decree to regulate slavery in the French Empire. This would be known as the Code Noir. As part of the code, France forced its slaves to convert to Roman Catholicism. To further their mission to spread the Catholic faith, the Code Noir also forced the expulsion of Jews who resided in the areas claimed by France.

The Code Noir had sixty articles. The code covered everything from how the slaves lived to the religion they practiced. It outlined how the slaves could be treated by their masters and how the slaves should be punished if any laws were broken.

We won't examine every article of the Code Noir, but let's look at a few of them. Article 9 of the Code Noir stated that children born to married slaves would also be slaves. However, if the married couple had separate masters, the child would belong to the female's master.

Article 13 said that children born to a slave father and a free mother would be given "free status" like their mother. However, if the father was free and the mother was a slave, the child would be a slave.

The code forbade slaves from possessing weapons. Slaves who violated this law would be punished by whipping, and their weapons would, of course, be confiscated. Slaves could have weapons that were used for hunting, although they had to be supervised by their masters.

Slaves were not allowed to sell goods, such as sugarcane, without the permission of their masters. Any illegal sale of goods would lead to a fine for the buyers. If a slave was sick, the master was required to pay for the slave's care while they were hospitalized.

According to Article 33, if a slave were violent toward their master or their master's family or mistresses, the slave would be put to death. Article 34 stated that fugitive slaves would have their ears cut off and be branded if they were on the run for more than a month after their master reported them missing. Subsequent violations of the article would lead to more severe punishment, including death after the third violation.

Slaves could not marry each other without the permission of their masters. The slaves also had to consent as well. Slaves that were married could not be separated from each other.

The Code Noir decreed that slaves were subject to more severe punishments than domestic servants. Soldiers of the French Empire were subject to less severe punishments for breaking laws. Thus, like elsewhere in the Caribbean and around the world, slaves were abused and mistreated under this code.

Despite the Code Noir forbidding masters from abusing, injuring, or killing their slaves for no reason, they were still given authority to discipline their slaves as they saw fit. Masters were rarely, if ever, convicted for murdering or torturing their slaves.

Masters had the power to manumit (free) their slaves. Unlike some of the other colonial laws that treated freed slaves poorly, France provided the same rights and privileges to freed slaves as French citizens. Of course, prejudices still existed, but freed slaves were allowed to own their own businesses and choose their own careers. They could even own slaves if they wanted to. Freed slaves did not need letters of naturalization to be granted citizenship.

It must be noted that freed slaves were not able to enjoy complete freedom. For instance, it was often difficult to raise a family. The children would be given the same status as their mother, so if a male freed slave had a child with an enslaved woman, their child would still be a slave.

In 1660, the first census for the island of Martinique took place. There were nearly 5,300 people who lived on the island; the whites only outnumbered the black slaves by about 100. Over the next twenty years, the number of slaves who inhabited the island grew to over fourteen thousand, while the white population lagged far behind. Overall, more than two-thirds of the population of Martinique by 1680 were black slaves.

With slaves outnumbering the whites, rebellions were a common threat. Yet, many rebellions were thwarted, with those responsible being punished harshly and even executed.

The Haitian Slave Revolt and Independence

Saint-Domingue was a French Caribbean colony. This meant the Declaration of the Rights of Man and of the Citizen, which declared all French men as free and equal, was applicable to the colony. This declaration did not end slavery, but the principles greatly inspired the slaves on Saint-Domingue to rise up against their masters.

By this time, the African population in the Caribbean was growing to the point where it would soon outnumber the whites if it didn't already.

Free blacks in Saint-Domingue were looking to be given equality and the same rights and status as the French. Vincent Ogé, a wealthy aristocrat known for his role in the Bourbon regime, wanted free blacks to be given the right to vote as declared by the Declaration of the Rights of Man. After the governor of Saint-Domingue refused, Ogé orchestrated an insurgency in 1790. The revolt consisted of three hundred free men of color, with the people asking for the same voting rights as the wealthy plantation owners. Ogé would be captured and executed the following year.

Whites and free blacks would be embroiled in conflicts while the black slaves watched. But in 1791, the slaves finally had their own revolt. After a Vodou ceremony, the slaves killed their owners, sparking a civil war.

The slaves fought back against their white oppressors. Masters and their family members and mistresses were forced out of their beds; many were killed. Plantations were set on fire, including two near the major cities of Jacmel and Léogâne.

More than two million francs in property damage had been inflicted. However, surviving whites formed a militia and fought back, killing as many as fifteen thousand rebel slaves.

The French abolished slavery in 1793. The slaves had scored a major victory. Black men who resided in French colonies were given political and civil rights. Since the revolution did not focus on women's rights, the Declaration of the Rights of Woman and of the Female Citizen would be published on September 14th, 1791, by Olympe de Gouges. Although this document did not lead to anything significant (besides her execution), it did begin the discussion of what women's rights might look like.

Although the French had abolished slavery, news traveled slowly. Toussaint Louverture, a leader of the Haitian Revolution, continued to fight alongside the Spanish. In 1794, he turned against Spain and fought with the French upon hearing about France's emancipation decree.

A former slave, Louverture became the governor-general of Saint-Domingue (Haiti) in 1797. Napoleon Bonaparte, who took power in 1799, felt threatened by Louverture's rise to power and forbade him from invading Santo Domingo, which would have placed the latter in a more powerful position. Louverture ignored

Napoleon and moved ahead with the plan.

Louverture wanted to establish his own vision of politics in the Caribbean. He captured Santo Domingo (the Dominican Republic) from Don Garcia, the governor at the time. He abolished slavery and afterward took control of Hispaniola.

In 1801, the citizens of Saint-Domingue were notified by Napoleon that France would create a constitution that included special laws for its colonies. Louverture decided to form a constitutional assembly of his own, consisting of white planters.

Louverture did not declare Saint-Domingue to be a free and independent state. He stated that it was a single colony that belonged to the French Empire. But he also stated that those who were born, lived, and died in Saint-Domingue would die as French subjects.

Napoleon dispatched his brother-in-law, General Charles Leclerc, to seize Hispaniola by diplomatic means in 1801. Louverture planned to burn down coastal cities and the plains to make it difficult for Leclerc and his forces to access supplies. He also relied on the possible spread of yellow fever to sicken and eventually kill the Leclerc's men.

Louverture was arrested in 1802. He would die while incarcerated at Fort de Joux at the age of sixty in 1803.

In 1802, Napoleon sent 5,200 members of a Polish legion to fend off prisoners who were rebelling. By this point, eight thousand men under Leclerc's command were ready to fight, while ten thousand had died of yellow fever.

The Poles were shocked to discover they were actually sent to Saint-Domingue to fight rebelling slaves. Although the Poles were fighting with France to gain their independence, many were so moved by the slaves' cause that they turned on Napoleon and sided with the slaves. The Poles who fought alongside the slaves were granted Haitian citizenship for their efforts once the country became independent.

In 1803, the French were losing their grip on the colony and began to focus on other enemies, such as Prussia and Great Britain.

After the French forces were defeated by the Haitian rebels, they left Hispaniola by the end of 1803. The beginning of 1804 marked the official inception of Haiti; the name was inspired by Ayiti, its original indigenous name. The Haitian Revolution was the only slave revolt in history that led to an independent state run by non-whites. Haiti was also the first country in the Western Hemisphere to end slavery.

However, the Haitian Revolution was bloody and violent. And this violence did not end with the war. In 1804, the Haitians carried out a massacre to kill any remaining French colonists. Thousands of people were killed.

English Slave Laws

The Code Noir drew inspiration from the English colonies, as England had already passed slave codes of its own, including the Barbados Slave Code of 1661.

The Barbados Slave Code

The Parliament of Barbados passed a slave code in 1661. This allowed masters to have full authority over how they could control and treat their slaves without worrying about any legal repercussions. The Barbados Slave Code also applied to the other British colonies in the Caribbean, including Jamaica and even some of the colonies in what would become the United States.

At the outset, the Barbados Slave Code was designed to serve both the slaves and their masters. However, these plans failed, as the protections did not go far enough to ensure the slaves were treated humanely.

For instance, the code stated slaves should be provided with a change of clothes annually. But the code did not detail what a slave's diet should be or if the slave owners needed to provide adequate housing. The slave code certainly favored slave owners. According to the Barbados Slave Code, slave owners had the authority to punish their slaves if they committed infractions. The slave code also gave slave owners permission to use other means of bodily harm, such as branding, whipping, lacerating, or even crippling or murdering them. Some of the slave owners even set their slaves on fire as a severe punishment.

Slave owners would not face any kind of legal consequences for their treatment of slaves. English common law did not provide the right to a jury or a judge to Africans who were free or enslaved.

In the 1780s, the code underwent reforms, which resulted in an increase in the slave population. Despite the amendments, the working and living conditions of slaves never improved.

Slavery in the Dutch Colonies

In 1644, the Netherlands passed a legal code regarding slavery that applied to its colonies, including those in the Caribbean. Before it was enacted, slaves in the Dutch colonies were baptized by the Dutch Reformed Church.

The island of Curaçao served as a transfer port for slaves, as most of them would be sent to Dutch colonies in South America. In 1789, the island had nearly thirteen thousand slaves, which was over triple the number of whites on the island.

In 1795, the island witnessed a slave uprising involving forty to fifty slaves. They left a plantation owned by Caspar Lodewijk van Uytrecht. They told van Uytrecht they no longer regarded themselves as slaves. Van Uytrecht told the slaves to take up their issue with the lieutenant governor of Curaçao.

A slave named Tula headed the rebellion and led the slaves to Lagún, where they released some prisoners. The slaves continued to travel, freeing people as they went.

Van Uytrecht commissioned his son to send a message to the governor of Curaçao about the slave revolt. The Dutch navy and military were dispatched to confront Tula and the rebels.

However, the Dutch military was defeated. Tula and those following him were surely a force to be reckoned with. Tula issued demands to the government: Sundays off, full freedom to purchase clothing and other items, and the end of collective punishment. Although his demands were fairly lenient, the Europeans did not want to give any freedom to the slaves. The rebels were defeated after Baron Westerholt, who attempted several negotiations with the rebels beforehand, ordered that any slave with weapons should be shot.

A skirmish took place, resulting in nine rebel deaths and twelve arrests. Those who escaped began to enact guerilla warfare against the Dutch. Tula was captured and tortured to death on October 3rd, 1795. He is remembered as a national hero in Curaçao for leading the revolt.

The colonial government didn't want another revolt, so it granted enslaved people some rights, although it's not specified what rights these were.

Nearly one thousand years later, in 1863, Curaçao abolished slavery around the same time as the Netherlands. At the time, nearly 5,500 slaves resided on the island.

Final Thoughts

The slave laws of the Caribbean colonies cleared the way for slave owners to mistreat their slaves. Many slaves suffered brutality on an unprecedented scale and also suffered from various diseases, with many of them dying. The French were the first to abolish slavery in the Caribbean, although it was reinstated by Napoleon in 1802, making its abolition a short-lived affair.

Let's not forget who truly abolished slavery first in the Western Hemisphere. Haiti abolished the institution of slavery and became the second independent nation in the Americas, with the United States being the first. Haiti would witness many years of conflict throughout the remainder of the 19th and 20th centuries.

The colonial slave laws in the Caribbean inspired many rebellions, as the slaves were tired of suffering inhumane torture and violence at the hands of slave owners.

Chapter 5 – Revolutions in the Caribbean

The Caribbean had long been the backdrop of many violent conflicts. Wars that had ignited in the European mainland would eventually make their way to the Caribbean shores. The European powers would even turn on the pirates who had aided them against the countries they warred against.

The 18th century witnessed two of the most notable revolutions in world history: the American and French Revolutions. The Caribbean region served as a theater for these revolutionary wars.

From the 1770s to the 1790s, the Caribbean settlements played vital roles in revolutions that created new nations. This chapter will cover the events of the American and French Revolutions, as well as notable events that happened in the Caribbean during both wars.

The American Revolution

By the mid-1700s, the colonists of British America already had a form of autonomy, as each of the Thirteen Colonies was governed by its own legislature. However, the people were still beholden to laws passed by the British Parliament.

The American colonists had no direct representation in Parliament, so the citizens had no one to speak up for their rights and dissatisfaction with the laws. Some people in Britain, including those in Parliament, were sympathetic to the colonists, but many didn't understand why the colonists didn't want to be part of the motherland. The British had invested time and money in the colonies, so they believed they should have the ultimate say in what happened in the American colonies.

The British also wanted to reap the benefits of the prosperous American economy. After fighting so many wars in Europe, Britain needed to replenish its coffers, especially since it seemed as if more wars were on the horizon. The British had sent men to aid the colonists in the French and Indian War. In their eyes, they had defended the territory with their men and money, so they deserved to be repaid. This led to the Stamp Act of 1765. The law was aimed at taxing many printed items that were created in the colonies, including newspapers and official documents.

The Stamp Act was repealed about a year later. The American colonists' anger played a large role in its appeal; the Stamp Act led to the famous phrase "No taxation without representation," and many people boycotted products. However, the peace would not last long, as the Townshend Acts would be passed in 1767. With tensions rising in large cities such as Boston, British soldiers were deployed to calm things down.

In 1770, the Boston massacre occurred. Five colonists were killed, exacerbating tensions between the British and Americans. Around the same time, many of the taxes of the Townshend Acts were repealed. However, the tax placed on tea was retained, further angering the colonists. And the Tea Act of 1773, which was to help cut down on smuggling and bail the British East India Company out, triggered the Boston Tea Party. Colonists dumped almost ten thousand pounds' worth (two million dollars today) of tea into Boston Harbor.

As a result, Britain passed the Intolerable Acts, which shut down Boston Harbor until the colonists paid back the tea and effectively put Massachusetts under the control of the British, among other things. The Intolerable Acts were, well, intolerable, and the following year, 1774, twelve colonies (with the exception of Georgia) responded by forming the Continental Congress.

Of course, not all of the colonists wanted independence. Britain provided security, and many felt a sense of loyalty to the motherland. The Loyalists or Tories were up against the vociferous

Patriots, who opposed British rule to the point they were willing to go to war for independence.

Citizen militias formed to confront the British forces, and fighting began in Lexington and Concord on April 19th, 1775. The Continental Army, which was led by George Washington, was formed soon after.

Several battles took place within the year. For instance, the siege of Boston saw the Americans regain the city. On July 4th, 1776, the Continental Congress declared America to be an independent nation and adopted the Declaration of Independence. The Declaration of Independence rejected the monarchy, replacing it with a republic that promoted liberty and freedom.

Throughout the years, the newly formed United States would engage Great Britain's large military force in many battles. While the Americans were beaten badly at the beginning, they gained strength and began to turn things around. Their turning point was their victory against the British in the Battle of Saratoga in 1777.

Due to their victory, France became America's ally, providing supplies and manpower. The war for independence eventually cemented the republic's status as an independent nation. The ideals of what the Americans fought for spread to France, which kicked off the French Revolution. But before we head to France, let's see how the Caribbean was impacted by the revolution in America.

The American Revolution in the Caribbean

Great Britain had around thirty colonies in the Americas at this time. However, the British considered Jamaica their crown jewel, as it was one of the wealthiest colonies due to the sugar trade. Aside from Jamaica, Britain also had Barbados, Dominica, Saint Vincent, Tobago, and the Leeward Islands.

Bermuda was another British colony off the coast of America. It was the only colony outside of the mainland to send representatives to the Continental Congress, although Bermuda was not looking to be included in the United States. The delegates sought an exemption from the trade ban the Americans planned to enact.

Although representatives from Caribbean colonies did not attend, the British Caribbean colonies would play essential roles in the American Revolution. British colonies were used as shipping channels for military supplies for the navy and soldiers on the ground.

Meanwhile, the French and Dutch were aligned with the Continental Army. Like Britain, they used their island colonies to assist the Americans by providing them with military supplies. Colonial privateers attempted to undermine Britain's economy by destroying any ships that were in the vicinity.

While most of the conflicts happened on land and in the seas north of the Caribbean, some revolutionary conflicts did occur near the islands. The first conflict occurred in 1776 when privateers attacked The Bahamas. In 1777, the privateers set their sights on Tobago and laid siege to the island colony on two separate occasions.

The island nation of Saint Croix, then claimed by the Danish, confirmed its alliance with the Americans by saluting its flag. Fort Orange, on the island of Sint Eustatius, noticed an American ship sailing by and confirmed its alliance by doing the same in the latter half of 1777.

General William Howe, one of the key commanders of the British Army, relied on the Jamaican and Barbadian colonies to provide troops and supplies. His requests were barely met, though. Troops in Jamaica had their hands tied due to a separate conflict, as a number of slaves revolted. Barbados was only able to send food to Howe and his troops, even though the colony was suffering from widespread famine.

The Leeward Islands relied on food that was imported from British America. The importation of food was disrupted due to the war to the point where one-fifth of Antigua's slave population had died of famine.

Meanwhile, American privateers were holed up on islands claimed by France and the Netherlands. Their role included finding supplies and sending them to the Continental Army.

In 1779, Spain joined the Revolutionary War by aiding the American colonists with money and supplies. By this point, the British navy was stretched thin. Aside from defending their interests in the Americans and the Caribbean, their remaining navy was doing the same in parts of Asia and the Mediterranean.

In 1781, the British surrendered at Yorktown, Virginia, which marked the end of most of the fighting. The American Revolution would be officially over in 1783 with the Treaty of Paris. The British would cede control of its colonies east of the Mississippi River and south of the Great Lakes to the United States.

The British colonies in the Caribbean and Canada were the only claims Britain had left in America.

The French Revolution

In France, social and economic equality was lacking, and the people were not happy. The population had grown, and there were financial issues from assisting the United States in its revolution. And on top of this, agricultural issues and high food prices were exacerbating tensions between the average French person and the incredibly wealthy.

In 1789, the Estates General was called to meet for the first time in almost two centuries. The delegates of the assembly were responsible for listing grievances that would be submitted to the king. When it was about to convene, a debate ensued over the voting process. As a result, the Third Estate, the largest group, which represented the commoners, decided to meet separately and create the National Assembly.

The Third Estate intended to convene in its usual meeting place in Versailles. However, its members were locked out. It was assumed the king wanted the group to disband, but they were not deterred. Instead, they met at an indoor tennis court.

There, the Third Estate took an oath. They promised not to separate until a constitution was written and established. In August of 1789, they created what was known as the Declaration of the Rights of Man and of the Citizen, which was intended to provide individual liberty and democracy to France.

King Louis XVI dismissed his financial minister Jacques Necker, who supported the Third Estate, on July 11th. News of this angered the Parisian citizens. They also feared an attack by the royal army or other mercenaries that worked for the king.

On July 14th, 1789, French insurgents stormed a fortress named the Bastille to procure weapons, marking the beginning of the French Revolution. This would lead to the eventual deposition and execution of King Louis XVI, who was arrested in August 1792. His wife, Marie Antoinette, was executed in October 1793.

The rise of democratic principles would lead to the abolition of the monarchy and the subsequent establishment of the First French Republic. It would also lead to a bloody time in history known as the Reign of Terror and the rise of Napoleon Bonaparte, a military dictator who rolled back many of the democratic principles that had been gained.

The Effects of the French Revolution on the Caribbean

Planters in Martinique felt the effects of the French Revolution to the point where they had to relocate to Trinidad with their slaves as early as 1789. They continued to grow sugar and cocoa.

In April 1792, the Legislative Assembly extended French citizenship to free men of color. Donatien-Marie-Joseph de Vimeur, Vicomte de Rochambeau, was dispatched to Martinique to apply the law. The Constitutional Assembly on the island agreed to promulgate it.

However, Martinique was placed under the authority of Great Britain in 1793 after an accord was signed in London. This was a temporary arrangement until the monarchy in France was reestablished, as the British feared revolutionary fervor would spread to their Caribbean colonies. This accord also gave French colonists the right to continue enslaving people.

When France abolished slavery in 1794, Great Britain stepped in. It invaded the island to prevent the implementation of the decree from ever happening.

The islands of Martinique and Guadeloupe would be returned to France in 1802, only for the British to retake them again in 1809. They were restored to the French in 1814.

The Napoleonic Wars in the Caribbean

The Napoleonic Wars lasted from 1803 to 1815 and were fought throughout much of Europe and abroad. One campaign was in the West Indies, which began in 1803. By this point, France had already lost colonies in the Americas, including Haiti and Louisiana via the Louisiana Purchase. However, they maintained the colonies of Martinique and Guadeloupe.

In 1795, the French were able to force Spain to cede control of Santo Domingo to them in accordance with the Treaty of Basel.

In 1804, the British had established themselves on Diamond Rock, an uninhabited island near Martinique. The French planned to launch a nighttime assault on the rock. Sea conditions denied the French Navy the opportunity to attack, and the French went back to Martinique empty-handed. But the battle for the rock was not over yet. The French and British would exchange gunfire on May 14th, 1805.

The French were aided by the Spanish in their efforts to fight the British. On May 31st, the French launched a final attack. It was clear the British could not sustain the assault, and the British surrendered on June 2nd.

The next major battle in the Caribbean would occur on February 6th, 1806, with the Battle of Santo Domingo. The British fought the French in the waters near the colony. The British Royal Navy was a formidable force, and the French suffered over 1,500 casualties. Over a thousand men were captured.

Perhaps the two biggest battles in the Caribbean during the Napoleonic Wars were the invasions of Martinique in 1809 and Guadeloupe in 1810.

The invasion of Martinique began when Vice Admiral Sir Alexander Cochrane and Lieutenant General George Beckwith led a large expeditionary force of ten thousand men and twenty-nine ships to Martinique. Great Britain saw the French occupation of Martinique as a threat to its trade prospects in the Caribbean.

The British landed on the southern and northern coasts and defeated the French forces stationed there. They officially controlled the island on February 24th, 1809. The French tried to send reinforcements to regain the island but were intercepted by the British in April 1809.

With Martinique in British hands, their next target was Guadeloupe. Beckwith and Cochrane gathered their forces and departed Dominica on January 27th, 1810. The British sent messages to the French occupying the island, telling them to surrender.

Upon receiving the message, General Jean Augustin Ernouf and his remaining troops decided to stay and guard the island. However, the British forces overwhelmed Ernouf and the French, thanks to the aid of British reinforcements led by General Charles Wale.

The Napoleonic Wars would end on November 20th, 1815, months after Napoleon's defeat at Waterloo.

Final Thoughts

The Caribbean served as a theater for wars for many years. It witnessed the effects of three revolutionary wars and a continental war. These wars changed the European political landscape.

France regained the islands of Martinique and Guadeloupe after the Napoleonic Wars. They are both considered overseas departments of France today.

Chapter 6 – The Caribbean in the 19ᵗʰ Century: War for Cuban Independence and the Spanish-American War

With the American and French Revolutions in the rearview mirror, the Caribbean still found itself under the control of European powers. Napoleon was overthrown, but another power player emerged in the region. The United States of America would soon establish itself as a nation with interests beyond its borders.

This chapter will cover the events of the Caribbean beginning from the early 19ᵗʰ century up until the beginning of the Spanish-American War, which was fought at the end of the century. The Spanish-American War would be Spain's last attempt at retaining what it had left in the region, including lands it had held on to for three centuries.

Haiti would declare its independence. In the years that followed, other nations, including the Dominican Republic and Cuba, would join the fray.

The Monroe Doctrine

On December 2ⁿᵈ, 1823, US President James Monroe issued the Monroe Doctrine, which outlined America's foreign policy.

Monroe created four pillars that would determine the country's intent on how it would deal with foreign affairs.

Monroe believed both the Old and New Worlds were different in terms of the systems they operated on and that it must stay that way. The Monroe Doctrine included the following points:

- The United States would not get involved with wars between European powers. It would also stay out of the internal affairs of Europe.

- All existing colonies claimed by European nations would be recognized by the United States. They would not face any kind of interference from America.

- There would be no further colonization in the Western Hemisphere.

- Controlling or oppressing a nation located in the Western Hemisphere would be considered an act of hostility against the United States.

By this time, some European nations had territorial interests in the United States, such as Russia, whose focus was on the northwestern coast of the US, such as parts of present-day Oregon and Washington State. The Monroe Doctrine aimed to end those territorial ambitions.

The British wished to create a joint declaration with the United States to further prevent colonization in the Americas. However, the US was not interested. The Monroe Doctrine fell on deaf ears outside of the United States (except for Britain) due to the fact that the US had no plans to colonize.

Great Britain must have gotten tired of being the only nation to uphold the doctrine. Ten years after the Monroe Doctrine was issued, Great Britain occupied the Falkland Islands off the coast of Argentina. The United States did not invoke the Monroe Doctrine at this time, nor did it voice its opposition to the occupation.

During James K. Polk's term as president, he made it clear that Great Britain and Spain were not allowed to establish colonies on the American mainland or the Yucatán Peninsula of Mexico. In other words, territorial expansion by the Europeans was out of the question. It was territory claimed by the United States. The Monroe

Doctrine did not affect the British colonies in the Caribbean since they were already recognized as sovereign nations.

With the British presence strong in the Caribbean, there were concerns regarding America's intent to use the Caribbean as a strategic area for its military and economic interests. In the US, many business owners in the North and slave owners in the South agreed that American expansion was vital. However, there was a concern regarding slavery.

Some opposed the idea of expansion, criticizing it as an opportunity to expand slavery in the United States. The idea of filibustering was on the table. Filibustering is defined as seizing land from foreign entities via military forces without any prior approval from the United States government.

Slave owners hoped that Cuba, Mexico, and other parts of the Caribbean would be successfully seized so they could acquire more slaves to work the lands. However, there was worry that a revolution in Cuba would take place in the same manner as it did in Haiti.

Despite America's attempts to purchase Cuba, the annexation of the Caribbean country, which is located nearly ninety miles off the coast of South Florida, never happened.

The American Civil War and the Caribbean's Role

The American Civil War began in 1861 and ended in 1865. It pitted the Union against the Confederacy, with the two sides fighting over slavery and other ideological and economic issues.

At the time, The Bahamas was under British authority but became involved in the American Civil War. Blockade runners who had pledged their allegiance to the Confederates holed up in The Bahamas during the war.

Blockade runners dealt with major challenges during the war, namely the lack of ports in Florida, which was fairly close to Nassau. Since Florida was not accessible, blockade runners sailed to the largest Confederate port: Charleston, South Carolina. They made regular trips from Nassau to Charleston, fending off any Union forces at sea while importing cotton back to the Caribbean islands. While the blockade runners were active, the population on Grand Bahama Island doubled.

Nassau became an important trade port for the Confederacy. The cotton that was brought from Charleston was moved to cotton mills owned by Great Britain. The British recognized the Confederate States of America as being at war with the Union but did not recognize it as a sovereign nation. Instead of recognizing a side, Great Britain maintained its neutrality, but the public certainly had their own opinions. Many upper-class Brits supported the Confederates, while the middle and lower classes had a favorable opinion of the Union.

In 1861, Confederate President Jefferson Davis appointed two commissioners in an effort to generate foreign interest, namely from Great Britain and France. John Slidell and James Mason made the trip to Cuba, where they awaited the arrival of the RMS *Trent*, a British mail ship.

During this time, word that the pair were planning to hitch a ride on the *Trent* reached Captain Charles Wilkes of the USS *San Jacinto*. The *San Jacinto* intercepted the *Trent*, and the two Confederate men were captured. No one was harmed, and the Union believed it had acted appropriately. Stopping a neutral ship during wartime was not seen as an act of violence against the ship's country of origin. But the British did not see it the same way. Because of the aggression, Britain sent troops to Canada and threatened a blockade near New York City if an armed conflict between the Union and Great Britain broke out.

Britain would soon place an embargo on saltpeter, which was a major ingredient for gunpowder. At the time, the British Empire controlled more than 90 percent of its supply. President Lincoln responded by having Slidell and Mason released from prison and sent a half-hearted apology to the British, which they accepted.

The Cuban War of Independence and the Spanish-American War

The island nation of Cuba wanted to gain its independence. Its first attempt was in 1868, when Cuban rebels went to war with Spain in what would be known as the Ten Years' War. At this point, Cuba and Puerto Rico were the last two Spanish colonies in the Caribbean.

When slavery was abolished in Cuba in 1886, change swiftly came. Sugar mills dwindled in numbers, and only the most powerful landowners could stay in business.

At this time, writer and political activist José Martí resided in the United States after being deported to Spain for a second time. He planned a revolutionary movement with Cuban exiles to fight for Cuba's independence.

The United States wanted to annex Cuba for its own interests, but Martí was against the annexation efforts. On Christmas Day, 1894, three Cuban revolutionary ships left Florida for Cuba. Two of them were seized by the United States government, yet the Cuban revolutionaries moved forward with their plan.

In March 1895, Martí issued the Manifesto of Montecristi. This was the blueprint for the Cuban War of Independence. Some of the tenets outlined in the manifesto stated that both whites and blacks needed to participate to win the war. Revolutionaries should spare Spanish colonists who didn't object to their cause.

Martí and the revolutionaries wanted to bring economic prosperity to an independent Cuba. On February 24th, 1895, the violence began, and uprisings took place in major Cuban cities. The Cubans had nearly fifty-four thousand troops, but Spain had nearly four times the strength.

The rebels (known as mambises) faced several challenges besides their numerical disadvantage. For instance, they only had a small number of weapons. This was due to the ban on weapons after the Ten Years' War had ended. To mitigate this, the rebels captured ammo and weapons from the Spanish military during raids.

To the mambises' credit, they used guerilla warfare tactics and the element of surprise to their advantage. They would ride on horses and use machetes in their battles with Spanish soldiers. The rebels suffered a major loss when Martí was killed on May 19th, 1895, during the Battle of Dos Rios.

The rebels soon faced off against the forces led by Spanish General Arsenio Martínez-Campos y Anton, known for his efforts in the Ten Years' War. He was governor of Cuba before being replaced by General Valeriano Weyler in 1896 for refusing to engage in harsher tactics against the Cubans.

Weyler wasted no time with his plan to retaliate for Spanish losses. Unlike his predecessor, he was not afraid to get his hands bloody. He implemented a Reconcentration Policy that was designed to imprison Cubans in concentration camps. He ordered citizens of rural towns to move to the camps located in nearby fortified cities or face execution.

Within the next two years, a third of the Cuban population was confined in these camps. Unfortunately, between 150,000 and 400,000 died due to starvation and disease. Because of the countless people that suffered, Weyler was given the nickname "The Butcher" by the American newspapers.

Toward the end of the 1890s, Spain had its hands tied in its efforts to retain other colonies abroad, including the Philippines.

In January 1898, Cubans loyal to Spain started a riot in Havana. The United States sent the USS *Maine* to the Cuban capital to protect Americans living there. On February 15th, 1898, the *Maine* exploded, killing 260 on board.

Back then, newspapers ran with the story that the *Maine* had exploded because of a mine, but it seems more likely that something happened inside the ship. Most investigators believe the ammunition stocks caught on fire. Nevertheless, the incident kicked off the Spanish-American War, which began in late April 1898. The United States invaded Cuba, the Philippines, Guam, and Puerto Rico.

The first United States force arrived in Cuba on June 10th, 1898. Two weeks later, the Fifth Army Corps landed in areas east of Santiago.

On July 25th, the United States made landfall in Puerto Rico with about 1,300 soldiers under the command of Nelson A. Miles. This led to the Battle of Yauco and later the Battle of Fajardo. The final battle in Puerto Rico was held near Cerro Gervasio del Asomante, after which an armistice between the United States and Spain was signed.

Spain's grip weakened, and it requested peace months after the Spanish-American War began. On August 12th, Spain and the United States signed a peace agreement that included surrendering Cuba and Puerto Rico. The Treaty of Paris was signed that December, in which Spain officially recognized Cuba as an independent nation.

Puerto Rico was annexed by the United States as a territory, and US forces continued to occupy Cuba. Although the US did not permanently occupy Cuba, it made sure that Cuba's new legislative policies favored the US.

However, one of their military installations was still in place: Guantanamo Bay Naval Base, which was created as part of a 1903 lease agreement.

Final Thoughts

Spain's presence in the Caribbean no longer existed after the Spanish-American War, although its influence can still be felt in the culture and language of the countries it once occupied.

Cuba became an independent nation but would soon see itself at the forefront of global politics less than a half-century later. In regards to the Caribbean, the United States gained Puerto Rico, which remains a US territory to this day (along with the US Virgin Islands, but more on that later).

The Monroe Doctrine served as a blueprint for preventing European powers from further colonizing the Western Hemisphere. However, a new foreign policy would be enacted at the start of the 20th century.

Chapter 7 – The Early 20th Century in the Caribbean

The Spanish-American War ended with Spain surrendering the last of its colonies in the Caribbean. Cuba became an independent nation, while the United States gained territorial control over Puerto Rico. At the start of the 20th century, President Theodore Roosevelt established his own foreign policy that focused on the Caribbean and Latin America.

The Caribbean region finally began to see peace. After centuries of on-and-off conflicts, the Caribbean islands were growing used to the status quo of being under the jurisdiction of their European nation. Great Britain claimed the lion's share of the region, while some of the other islands were under French and Dutch control.

By the early 20th century, many of the Caribbean islands had their own functioning basic services. For instance, many of the British-occupied islands had hospitals, firefighters, police officers, and schools. Slavery was no more, but blacks in the Caribbean were still looking to gain the same rights as their white counterparts.

Regardless, political stability was stronger than ever before, and the quality of life increased, which led to economic benefits. Seeing the prosperity of the region, America sought to establish its own economic interests in the tropical area. The Caribbean would soon become one of the most desirable places to travel.

Even though economic advances were being made, one industry started to decline. Sugar, which was once considered a major cash crop, was seeing a low point.

As the 20th century progressed, Caribbean citizens under the rule of the United Kingdom would find themselves involved in a faraway war called World War I.

The Roosevelt Corollary

When Theodore Roosevelt assumed the US presidency after his predecessor, William McKinley, was assassinated, one of his focal points was foreign policy. Specifically, he was concerned that European powers intended to invade Latin American nations, which were facing issues with debts. Roosevelt saw the Monroe Doctrine as being too passive for American foreign policy and wanted to update it.

During Roosevelt's first term, Europe repeatedly threatened to invade Latin America to settle debts with countries that had weak governments. In 1902, blockades were established by Great Britain, Germany, and Italy. The United States responded by using its navy, intending to play the role of mediator.

However, the same thing would occur in the Caribbean. The Dominican Republic, which gained independence from Haiti in 1844, faced the threat of invasion due to defaulting on its debts. Ulises Heureaux, president of the Dominican Republic from 1882 to 1899 (with some gap years between terms), brought the country into debt after he became involved with financial schemes with European nations while pocketing money for himself.

After Heureaux's assassination, the Dominican Republic was unable to repay its debts to France and Great Britain. As a result, warships from both nations made their presence known in the Caribbean. The United States saw this as a direct threat to its own economic and political interests.

The Roosevelt administration would soon take over the Dominican Republic's customs house, paying the foreign lenders a portion of the money that rolled into the country via trade goods.

In 1904, Roosevelt addressed Congress and introduced the Roosevelt Corollary. This was tied to the Monroe Doctrine and guaranteed that the United States would take action should any

European power invade Latin America. The corollary is considered to be one of the cornerstones of the United States, which established itself as an enforcer in foreign politics by invading other countries that did wrong, not only in Latin America but also the world.

The Roosevelt Corollary would be associated with Teddy Roosevelt's "Big Stick" policy. The name was earned by the proverb, "Speak softly, and carry a big stick." It is entirely possible that Roosevelt came up with the quote himself, although he attributed it to a proverb from West Africa.

In other words, the Roosevelt Corollary was another way for the United States to assert its dominance when it proved necessary to do so. The Roosevelt Corollary also justified America's intervention in Latin America, including the Caribbean nations of Cuba and the Dominican Republic.

The United States occupied the Dominican Republic in 1916. Since the Dominican Republic's independence in 1844, it had experienced the growing pains of becoming an independent country. It had undergone several changes of leadership and was over $30 million in debt. The US attempted to install a president that would submit to its authority but failed. So, it maintained control over the country through a military government.

During the occupation, they faced rebellions from Dominicans. As time passed, the occupation became unpopular in both the Dominican Republic and the United States.

President Warren Harding made the decision to withdraw US troops. In 1922, some of the troops moved out, with the last of them leaving the island in 1924.

Tourism and the Rise of the Caribbean Economy

The tourism industry of the Caribbean dates as far back as the late 1700s. It was believed to be a place for curative tourism (a place outside of one's home country where one can rest and recuperate from an illness). Notable travelers to the Caribbean include George Washington, who would become the first US president. In 1751, he traveled to Barbados with his half-brother Lawrence, who was suffering from tuberculosis. He was treated at Bush Hill House on the island. It did not help Lawrence, as he died a year later at

Mount Vernon, Virginia.

One of the greatest benefits of Barbados was that the threat of malaria was low to non-existent. Curative tourism would make its way to Nevis, where the Bath Hotel opened its doors in 1778.

The Bath Hotel is believed to be the first-ever hotel in the Caribbean. One of its best features was its hot springs. Throughout the 19th century, more hotels opened up across the region, such as the Royal Victorian Hotel in The Bahamas and Crane Beach in Barbados.

Back then, many travelers sailed to Barbados and other parts of the Caribbean by steamship. Wealthy Europeans often spent their winters in the Caribbean. Many of them traveled to the Caribbean colonies their homeland controlled.

British citizens especially flocked to Barbados and Jamaica. Wealthy French citizens traveled to Martinique, while the Dutch sailed to Curaçao. Cuba and The Bahamas became popular Caribbean destinations for Americans.

The Caribbean would see as many as 100,000 tourists in a calendar year by the late 1930s. Many tourists traveled for vacation and spent time on the beaches. With the Caribbean seeing a rise in the quality of life and no violent conflicts (at least for the most part), it saw opportunities to grow its tourism economy.

Tourism would soon rival other industries like sugar and bananas. The prices of these industries were not as competitive due to the passage of free trade policies. The Caribbean would see its tourism industry thrive, although there was a slowdown during World War II. But after World II, tourism rose again, with millions of people visiting the region annually by the 1960s. The Caribbean is still known for its breathtaking landscapes and beautiful year-round weather.

American possession of the Virgin Islands

America's interest in the Caribbean continued during the 1900s. In 1902, it attempted to purchase the Virgin Islands from Denmark.

The Danish government was not opposed to selling the colony to the United States. The Folketinget approved the sale by a vote of eighty-eight to seven, sending it to the Landstinget, the other chamber of the Danish Parliament.

The Landstinget believed it had enough votes to approve the sale. However, an elderly man was brought to the Landstinget by ambulance. Upon his arrival, the Landstinget vote was a deadlock; thus, the initial sale of the Virgin Islands failed.

The United States would wait another fifteen years before it finally acquired the islands and renamed them the US Virgin Islands. This time around, its intent was to purchase the islands due to the fear Germany might occupy Denmark during World War I. President Woodrow Wilson put together a treaty, and it was signed on January 16th, 1917.

In exchange for Denmark's transfer of the Virgin Islands, the United States paid $25 million in gold coin to the Danish. In 1934, the island territory began to use the US dollar, replacing the daler that was used in the Danish West Indies.

US Occupation of Haiti

In 1915, Haiti was suffering from political and economic instability, which eventually led to the assassination of Haitian President Vilbrun Guillaume Sam. The United States would remain in Haiti for the next nineteen years.

But why did the US want anything to do with Haiti in the first place? The United States wanted to use Haiti for militaristic and economic purposes. The US believed Haiti would be a great site for a naval base. US interest in Haiti dates back to 1868 when Andrew Johnson floated the idea of creating a base there. Throughout the 1880s and 1890s, the United States tried but failed to procure a lease that would allow it to add military forces to the Caribbean nation.

While the United States said that sending US troops to Haiti would prevent anarchy, the true motives were due to two reasons. The first was its intent to protect its assets in Haiti, and the second was because of concerns of a possible German invasion.

Haiti maintained diplomatic and economic ties with France at this time. Haiti was in debt, even though the French government had considerable power over its finances and trade policy. The United States had an issue with Haiti's ties with France and had increasing concerns over Germany doing business on the island as well.

US President Woodrow Wilson suggested the Constitution of Haiti should be rewritten and include acceptance of foreigners owning land. The proposal was rejected, and the Haitians drafted a constitution of their own, which did not satisfy the United States.

The United States ordered President Philippe Sudre Dartiguenave to dissolve the legislature after its members refused to adopt the constitution. Major Smedley D. Butler, who led the Marines occupying Haiti, forced the Senate to close using intimidation by gunpoint.

The United States installed presidents that benefited its interests, although wealthy mulatto and other influential Haitians also benefited. This would be a problem for the average Haitian, who wanted someone that represented their interests.

In late 1915, the Gendarmerie, an occupational force that consisted of Haitians and Americans, was formed. The United States Marines oversaw it. In addition to controlling the military, the United States also gained control over Haiti's finances.

During the US occupation of Haiti, the First and Second Caco Wars broke out. The First Caco War was sparked in 1915 by Haitian rebels (known as Cacos). The Cacos were upset over the US occupation and protested the reinstatement of the corvée (unpaid, forced labor) system, as they felt they were sliding backward to times of slavery. While there were few casualties on the American side, two hundred Caco rebels were killed.

The Second Caco War began in 1918, resulting in the loss of twenty-eight Americans and nearly seventy Gendarmes. The Caco rebels would lose nearly two thousand men. The Second Caco War proved to be much deadlier to the rebels, but it also helped bring the atrocities that were happening to light. However, the US Congress did not hear testimonies from Haitians and said the occupation was necessary for "chronic revolution, anarchy, barbarism, and ruin" to be avoided.

The US occupation of Haiti has been marred by controversy. The US established a military regime and suppressed Haitians who opposed it. The US was guilty of enforcing the corvée system on the Haitian people, as well as extrajudicial executions, censorship, and acts of racism. Around 15,000 Haitians were killed during the occupation, with at least 5,500 dying in labor camps alone.

Despite US involvement, Haiti's political stability never improved. With many Haitians in poverty, uprisings were led against the United States in 1929. This led to a conflict known as the Les Cayes massacre, which resulted in the deaths of anywhere from twelve to twenty-two Haitians after the Marines opened fire on peaceful protestors.

Soon, international pressure played a role in pushing the United States out of Haiti. As it was preparing its exit, it helped the Haitians by training them on how to operate their government. When President Franklin Delano Roosevelt became president in early 1933, the United States and Haiti agreed to end the occupation later that year in August. The last of the United States Marines left in 1934.

World War I in the Caribbean

When World War I broke out in Europe, the nations of the West Indies sent around sixteen thousand troops to fight for the Allies. The region procured manpower, ammunition, and funds for the war effort.

In France, conscription was in effect. This included citizens of the French Caribbean nations of Martinique and Guadeloupe.

After World War I, soldiers from the West Indies received awards for their service. These included well over thirty military crosses and five Distinguished Service Orders. The Caribbean was affected by the war. For instance, there was an oil boom in Trinidad, while Jamaica's shipping industry suffered due to lower imports and exports.

The Battle of the Caribbean (1941-1945)

The Caribbean saw action in World War II, though. Oil imports from the Caribbean and the Gulf of Mexico were sent to aid the Allies. The Axis Powers of Germany and Italy intended to stop that aid and disrupt supply lines. None of the Caribbean nations supported the Axis Powers, so none of them were willing to help the Axis achieve their goals in the Caribbean.

Operation Neuland started on February 16th, 1942. German U-boats launched several attacks against oil tankers near Aruba and Curaçao. Italian submarines were situated near the Lesser Antilles during the operation.

Operation Neuland was a successful victory for the Axis Powers. Yet, it would be one of the only major victories they achieved in the Caribbean.

The Nazis also attempted to attack Puerto Rico, but no damage was done. Still, U-boats continued to attack various Allied ships off the American coast as the years passed. Only seventeen submarines from the Axis Powers would be lost, while hundreds of Allied merchant ships were destroyed by Germany and Italy.

Despite losing Operation Neuland, the Allied forces would claim victory in the Pacific and Atlantic Theaters after the fall of the Axis Powers.

Final Thoughts

At the turn of the 20th century, the United States made it clear that the European powers were not to invade the Western Hemisphere and justified its interests in the Caribbean. It would gain footholds in the region by either occupying or acquiring territory. Today, the US occupation of the Caribbean is not always viewed in a positive light, as its past actions are sometimes seen as controversial.

Meanwhile, the British and French colonies supplied soldiers to fight on the front lines in Europe. The Caribbean would not see action in the First World War but would see it during the Second World War.

In WWII, the Axis Powers were dangerously close to American soil. However, their mission to disrupt supply lines failed, and the Allied forces were able to go on to defeat the Axis Powers.

Chapter 8 – Dictatorships in the Caribbean

By the end of the 19th century, some Caribbean nations had broken free from European powers to form their own independent states. They no longer wanted to live under the authority of government entities that were thousands of miles away.

On paper, it sounded as if the people of these independent nations wanted to live freely and by their own laws. However, as time passed, dictatorships became common in the Caribbean and other parts of Latin America. This chapter will cover the notable dictatorships of the late 19th and 20th centuries.

The Dominican Republic would see several dictators come and go, notably Ulises Heureaux and Rafael Trujillo. Those who opposed a dictatorship would often either flee or be executed. The authoritarian rule would soon become commonplace in the neighboring nations of Haiti and Cuba. The idea of free and independent states in the Caribbean didn't appear to be a possibility.

The Dominican Republic under Dictatorships

Pedro Santana

While one of the most notable dictators in the Dominican Republic was Trujillo, many of his predecessors ruled the eastern half of Hispaniola with an iron fist. While the Dominican Republic declared independence from Spain in 1821, it did not form its first republic until two decades later due to the annexation and occupation of Haiti.

In 1844, Pedro Santana claimed power as the first leader of the Dominican Republic. He was known for being a military leader but would rule as a dictator and eliminate anyone who opposed his authority. He also executed those who threatened him, including General Antonio Duvergé (along with his son), for charges of conspiracy.

He captured other political opponents and accused them of conspiracy as well. Santana's political opponents were often imprisoned, tortured, and executed. One of his notable victims was María Trinidad Sánchez, one of the creators of the Dominican Republic's first flag, who was executed by firing squad in 1845. She refused to give up the names of her co-conspirators who were planning to overthrow Santana's dictatorship.

Santana assumed power as the leader of the Dominican Republic on four different occasions. In 1861, Spain regained control over the country at Santana's request. After losing colonies in the Caribbean for the last half decade, Spain quickly took Santana up on his offer and reestablished its presence in the Caribbean.

Ulises Heureaux

Prior to his rise to power, Ulises Heureaux fought against Spain after the European nation annexed the Dominican Republic in 1861. He rose through the ranks and helped lead the overthrow of two different regimes. When General Gregorio Luperón assumed the presidency of the Dominican Republic, he gave authoritative powers to Heureaux since he did not want to spend his time in Santo Domingo.

Luperón's presidency lasted a year, and he was succeeded by Fernando Meriño, a Catholic priest. Heureaux would serve in the Meriño Cabinet as the interior minister. However, his power and influence eclipsed Meriño, and he would finally rise to power as president of the Dominican Republic on September 1ˢᵗ, 1882, when Merino transferred his duties.

During his first tenure, Heureaux exiled his former military comrade Luperón. He assumed power on three different occasions and executed those who opposed his authority.

Corruption became one of the hallmarks of the Heureaux regime. He arranged financial deals with European countries and pocketed millions of dollars for himself. This led to the country's financial ruin.

When Heureaux was assassinated in 1899, the Dominican Republic was too weak to repay the European powers. The United States, under President Theodore Roosevelt, would soon intervene.

Rafael Trujillo

Of the many dictatorships that occurred in the Caribbean (and the Americas in general), the Trujillo regime may have been the most prominent and even the most brutal. In 1916, the United States occupied the Dominican Republic due to several instances of unrest.

A young Trujillo was trained by the United States military and commissioned as an officer. In 1925, he was named the commander of the National Police. Two years later, he reconstituted it as an army under his authority.

In 1930, Trujillo began his rise to power when he made a deal with Rafael Estrella, a rebel leader. If Estrella could take over as acting president, he would allow Trujillo to run for election should a new one take place. Under the Estrella regime, Trujillo became the head of the police and military as part of the agreement. When a new election took place later that year, Trujillo ran for the presidency, with Estrella running as his vice president.

Trujillo used his militia and police forces to intimidate and harass his political opponents, leading to the other presidential candidates dropping out of the race. In the end, Trujillo and Estrada captured 99 percent of the vote—an outlandish amount.

Some say they received more votes than there were voters.

Trujillo became president in August 1930 and placed the country under martial law weeks after he took office. A brutal hurricane swept through the region and killed two thousand people. The capital city was so badly damaged that it had to be rebuilt.

After the rebuilding, Trujillo renamed the capital Ciudad Trujillo. He also requested that many of the landmarks and monuments be named after him. He succeeded in making the Dominican Republic a country ruled by only one political party, the Dominican Party.

Trujillo ordered government employees to contribute 10 percent of their salaries to the national treasury. Of course, people weren't happy about that, so Trujillo did his best to quell any dissent. Intimidation tactics were used across the country to get Dominicans who weren't part of the Dominican Party to join. Those who were part of the party were required to carry membership cards that "confirmed" their allegiance. Those who did not have a membership card could be arrested and charged with the crime of vagrancy.

As expected, those who opposed the Trujillo regime went missing and/or were executed. By 1934, Trujillo had no political opponents to challenge him. Still, he ensured that every election was rigged in his favor and made sure that no one could eclipse him in terms of power.

Trujillo would use his group known as "The 42" to round up anyone who opposed him. Opponents feared the sight of a Red Packard, also known as the "car of death." They knew this car would bring about their doom, for the people inside were likely rounding up people on an execution list that was maintained regularly by Trujillo.

Although the Dominican Party was the sole party in power, Trujillo once allowed an opposing political party to be created. Unbeknownst to the members of the newly created party, Trujillo used it as an opportunity to find out who was not loyal to him and had the members arrested and/or executed.

In 1938, Trujillo decided not to run for reelection, as the US presidents had set a precedent of a two-term limit. His chosen successor was Jacinto Peynado. Trujillo returned to public life but ran for reelection in 1942, citing US President Franklin Roosevelt's motive for running for president for a third term.

After Trujillo's return to power, he lengthened the term limit; instead of being four years, they would now be five. Trujillo served as president until 1952.

During his time as the dictator of the Dominican Republic, Trujillo was on peaceful terms with the United States. When he returned to the presidency in the 1940s, he declared his allegiance to the Allied forces in their efforts against Germany, Italy, and Japan. The Dominican Republic chose not to send its soldiers to the front lines.

Trujillo had hostile ties with many Latin American nations, especially Venezuela, Costa Rica, and Haiti. In 1937, he orchestrated a massacre, believing that the neighboring country was a safe haven for his political opponents. He ordered a massacre of Haitians who resided close to the Haitian border. As many as twelve thousand Haitians were killed, though the number is likely higher; the true death toll remains unknown to this day.

As a result of the Parsley massacre, the Dominican Republic was forced to pay reparations to the victims' families to avoid an international scandal. However, the $525,000 sent to Haiti never reached the victims' families due to the widespread corruption in the Haitian government.

By the late 1940s, Cuba had its sights set on invading the Dominican Republic and removing Trujillo from power. Many of the Dominicans who had fled would make their home in Cuba. One of those refugees was Juan Bosch. The Cuban government approved the idea of invading the Dominican Republic, but the plan fizzled out.

When Fulgencio Batista took over as Cuba's leader, Trujillo threw his support behind those who opposed him. However, he switched sides and provided Batista with financial support when Fidel Castro began to make gains. Trujillo's efforts to keep Batista in power would fail, as Castro took over as Cuba's leader in 1959.

Batista fled to the Dominican Republic in hopes that Trujillo would help him. Trujillo essentially made Batista prisoner but helped him escape to Portugal after Batista paid him millions of dollars.

When Castro took over Cuba, he accused Trujillo of provoking Cuba since the Dominican dictator was responsible for assisting Batista's escape. In response, Trujillo beefed up his defense spending. The Dominican military beat back Cuban hostility, but it was clear the Dominicans were unhappy with their ruler. Trujillo cracked down even harder on the people, especially students who had grown up under the repressive dictatorship.

On May 30th, 1961, Trujillo was assassinated in an ambush outside of Santo Domingo. His son, Ramfis, briefly held on to power, but he worked alongside new president Joaquín Balaguer to help liberate the country from the previous regime. Balaguer was a violent leader as well; around eleven thousand people disappeared or were killed on his orders. But he did make progressive reforms in the country, allowing the people to prosper in ways that weren't available before.

Rafael Trujillo was interred in the Dominican Republic but later exhumed and reinterred in Spain.

Of the positive things that occurred under the Trujillo regime, the Dominican Republic witnessed modernization, including the improvement of its infrastructure. Although his regime was brutal, the Dominican Republic enjoyed some peace and prosperity, especially when compared to previous years.

Cuba under Batista

Before Fulgencio Batista's rise to power, he commanded the Sergeants' Revolt that led to Gerardo Machado's overthrow.

The leadership of Cuba would change hands multiple times throughout the 1930s. Eventually, Batista became president, winning the 1940 election over Ramón Grau San Martín. It was the first election that took place under the new constitution.

Batista was supported by the Democratic Socialist Coalition and the Communist Party of Cuba. During his first term, Cuba sided with the Allied forces in World War II. Batista also passed many social reforms and economic regulations at home.

Batista's term ended in 1944, with Ramón Grau taking over after defeating Carlos Saladrigas Zayas, whom Batista wanted to take power. After leaving office, Batista lived in the United States and maintained homes in New York and Florida. Despite living in the United States, he remained active in Cuban politics.

Under Grau, Cuba prospered and became one of the wealthiest nations in Latin America. Afterward, Carlos Prío Soccarrás, who served as a minister under Grau, was elected in 1948.

Batista returned to Cuba to run for president in 1952. Given his unpopularity, he had virtually no chance of regaining his old job. However, he proved his doubters wrong in a forceful way. He gained power by way of a military coup on March 10th, 1952, canceling the elections. He forced Prío out of power, with the former president going into exile. Over two weeks later, the United States recognized Batista's government.

Under the new Batista regime, industrial workers' wages increased. However, around one-fifth of the workforce was unemployed.

Batista also established relationships with those involved with organized crime, allowing mob bosses and their associates to be given a safe haven in Cuba. Due to this, the drug trade established a foothold in the island nation. Batista profited from the trade and other illicit activities like gambling and prostitution.

In the 1950s, demonstrations and even coups against Batista began to flare up. It got to the point where Batista had members of the Cuban military purged if they were against him. His police force often tortured and killed those who created unrest in the cities. Many of Batista's opponents' corpses would be mangled and left in the streets to send a message to others. An open letter was issued in 1958 that called for Batista to be removed from power. It is thought that up to twenty thousand people were killed during Batista's time in power.

The unrest against Batista allowed the United States to intervene and supply the Cuban government with weapons. It opposed Castro seizing power due to his leftist sentiments. In 1958, the US announced it would no longer sell weapons to Cuba after Batista used napalm and other military equipment against his opponents.

Later that year, Cuban elections were scheduled to take place but were delayed until November because of Castro's call for a general strike. Castro and his supporters also planted numerous bombs in civilian parts of Cuba.

At the end of the year, Batista informed his officials that he intended to flee Cuba due to the overwhelming presence of Castro's supporters, although the Batista regime's inefficiency, brutality, and corruption certainly played a role in his exile. On January 1ˢᵗ, 1959, Batista left Cuba and went to the Dominican Republic. The following week, Fidel Castro celebrated the seizure of power in Havana.

Batista eventually sought asylum in Portugal with the help of Rafael Trujillo after both the United States and Mexico denied him entry. António Salazar, the president of Portugal, allowed Batista to live in the country under the condition that he would never get involved with the country's political affairs.

Batista lived in Portugal for his remaining years. Despite Castro's plans to assassinate him, Batista died of a heart attack in 1973 while in Spain. What happened to Cuba next led to long-standing diplomatic tensions with the United States.

Haiti: The Duvalier Regimes

Hispaniola was separated into two independent states: the Dominican Republic and Haiti. Both nations suffered brutal regimes. The last notable Caribbean dictators we will cover hailed from Haiti. The first was named François "Papa Doc" Duvalier. Before taking power, he worked as a physician.

Duvalier found himself immersed in the teachings of black nationalism and Vodou, which had been part of Haitian culture for many years. (Vodou is also known as Voodoo or Vodun; we have used the spelling that those in the Caribbean use the most.) He became the director general of the National Public Health Service, where he led anti-yaw (an infection of the bones and joints caused by a bacterium) campaigns sponsored by the United States. After the overthrow of President Dumarsais Estimé in 1950, Duvalier left the government.

A few years later, he began orchestrating the overthrow of the military junta led by Paul Magloire, who had himself overthrown Estimé. By this time, Duvalier had gone underground to avoid capture. When Magloire resigned in December 1956, Duvalier had gained enough popularity to be elected president the following year.

As Duvalier was settling in, he reduced the military's numbers while consolidating power. He thought it was best to keep the military small, considering its active role in the overthrow of leaders. To help compensate for the lack of military personnel, he put together a private police force known as the Tonton Macoute. Its job was to intimidate and kill anyone who opposed the Duvalier regime.

Duvalier had a heart attack in 1959 and placed his aide, Clément Barbot, the leader of the Tonton Macoute, in charge of the government while he recovered. Even though Duvalier had approved this, he was upset when he returned, accusing Barbot of crossing the line and trying to take control. Barbot was arrested and eventually released, after which he really did try to overthrow Duvalier. The Tonton Macoute ultimately killed Barbot in 1963.

Duvalier was notorious for manipulating elections. Even his first election is thought to have been tampered with, albeit not as heavily as his later elections. In 1964, Duvalier became president for life, winning an improbable 99.9 percent of the vote.

Duvalier allowed corruption to run rampant during his time in office. By 1963, Duvalier embodied a cult of personality throughout Haiti. Aside from his brutality, his regime was known for harassing members of the Catholic Church; for instance, he expelled foreign bishops from Haiti, which led to his excommunication.

Dissidents, including the educated populace, left the country. Many of them had worked in education and healthcare, resulting in the collapse of those systems. Duvalier also took it upon himself to seize land that was owned by peasants while pocketing hundreds of millions of dollars in taxes and money from other countries, including $15 million paid annually by the United States to fight famine and poverty in Haiti. Many Haitians died from starvation; famine was widespread since the peasants were unable to work on their farms.

It is believed that sixty thousand people died while Papa Doc Duvalier was in power. Many were executed because of their opposition to the regime. Others died due to starvation stemming from the famine that gripped the country.

By the early 1970s, Duvalier was in ill health. He died on April 21ˢᵗ, 1971, at the age of sixty-four. His son, nineteen-year-old Jean-Claude ("Baby Doc"), would become the youngest world leader at that time. Originally, Jean-Claude wanted the presidency to be granted to his older sister since he didn't want to assume power.

The younger Duvalier continued to employ the Tonton Macoute to fend off any opposition to the regime. However, he made some reforms. For instance, he released some of his father's political prisoners and lifted some policies that had censored the press.

During Baby Doc's time in power, he improved Haiti's relationship with the United States. Many of the country's issues carried on throughout his time in office, including famine. More Haitians fled the country for the United States, while others went to the neighboring Dominican Republic.

While Haitians found a new life in the United States, those who fled to the Dominican Republic were soon working under harsh conditions on the sugar plantations, being paid little for their services. However, in terms of human rights, Baby Doc was less of a threat compared to his late father.

When foreign aid was given to Haiti, Baby Doc pocketed most of the money for his own financial gain. The IMF (International Monetary Fund) awarded $22 million in aid to Haiti in 1980 to battle famine. Baby Doc and his family kept $16 million, and another $4 million was paid to the Tonton Macoute. The rest of the money was used to improve Haiti's infrastructure.

Middle-class and wealthy Haitians found themselves purchasing land that had long been inaccessible. In 1986, Baby Doc was forced to step down at the request of the Reagan administration. He and his family fled to France.

The Duvalier family left the island with much of the money they had stolen throughout their time in power. After twenty-five years, the younger Duvalier returned to Haiti, claiming to want to help with the country's reconstruction.

The money he had in his possession was frozen and soon claimed by the Haitian government when he was being investigated for criminal charges. Baby Doc died in Port-au-Prince on October 4ᵗʰ, 2014, of a heart attack.

Final Thoughts

Three major Caribbean nations wrote a sordid history on authoritarianism. Those who opposed it were imprisoned or killed. The policies enacted by these governments would kill thousands due to famine.

Many people left their old lives behind in search of new ones. It was hard for the people to stay, as the dictators made corruption one of their mainstays in an effort to retain power for as long as possible. The United States either aligned with them or opposed them, depending on the sentiment of the nation and whoever was in power.

Ironically, the dictators who were brutal in their own right would back the Allied forces against the totalitarian regimes in Europe and Japan. This was mostly due to their alliance with the United States. However, by the end of the 1980s, only one dictator in the Caribbean remained in power.

When Fidel Castro took control of Cuba, no one knew the kind of impact he would have on the world. The Caribbean soon became a place of concern, as the United States worried about how communism in Cuba would affect it and its allies.

Chapter 9 – Cuba under Castro and Communism in the Caribbean

While the dictatorships of Trujillo in the Dominican Republic and the Duvaliers in Haiti were blemishes in Caribbean history, one man would outlast both of them. Fidel Castro led an anti-Batista revolution throughout much of the 1950s and succeeded by overthrowing the government in 1959.

For the next half-century, Castro gained the support of many young people and lower-class Cubans due to his social reforms. However, the middle class, wealthy, and professionals opposed him and fled the country, with many going to the United States. In time, Castro found himself on the world stage by associating with the Soviet Union during the Cold War.

With Cuba and the Soviet Union aligned, concerns about communism in America's backyard began to grow. When Ronald Reagan took office, he had concerns that the Caribbean was going to be a "red lake."

Despite this, Castro remained a beloved figure throughout his life. Communism attempted to spread in the Caribbean but failed. It even got to the point where an armed conflict involving the United States occurred in Grenada.

The Castro Regime Begins

When 1959 began, Fidel Castro celebrated his long-awaited victory over the Batista regime. However, he wasn't president at first. Instead, he served as prime minister, beginning his two-decade-long term on February 16th. The change in government signaled the beginning of the end of diplomatic relations between the Caribbean island and the United States, a situation that would last for over fifty years.

The following April, Castro visited Washington to meet with President Dwight D. Eisenhower. However, Vice President Richard Nixon visited Castro instead, much to the latter's dismay. While Nixon thought Castro was a natural leader, he believed Castro didn't understand what communism meant and that he didn't have a sound strategy for rebuilding Cuba. (Castro repeatedly denied being a communist but embraced the label later in life. It is likely he was a communist since the time he took power in 1959, as he placed many Marxists in high positions and held communist-aligned beliefs.) Castro, on the other hand, had nothing good to say about the US vice president, who would become president in his own right ten years later.

Castro traveled throughout the Americas to earn funding for a proposed plan that would financially benefit Latin America. However, his efforts failed. At home, Castro passed reforms, including the First Agrarian Reform. The policy set a land cap and prohibited foreigners from buying land in Cuba.

The policy greatly benefited the Cuban peasants but alienated the wealthy landowners who had to give up their lands under the land cap. Castro's mother was a landowner and lost some of her farmlands under the policy. By 1960, Castro was successful in redistributing over 15 percent of the country's total wealth.

The agricultural policies led to the Cuban government confiscating land that had been owned and invested in by Americans. Wealthy Cubans who had already fled or would later flee the country also had their lands seized. The sugar and oil industries were also nationalized, upsetting many around the world due to foreign investments.

Castro promoted tourism in Cuba, particularly targeting African Americans to visit. His main selling point was that Cuba was a country free of racial discrimination, which appeared to be a shot at the United States for its segregation laws.

The Cuban prime minister liked to be in touch with the common people, and he began to speak to them directly via television and radio. He was popular with a majority of the population, namely the peasants and workers. The younger Cuban population was also big supporters of the Castro regime. But many professionals, such as doctors and engineers, were not fans of Castro. When they left, Cuba found itself in the midst of a brain drain.

Alliance with the Soviet Union

By 1960, Cuba had already aligned itself with the Soviet Union. Castro had developed severe anti-American sentiments and shared the same views as the Soviet Union and other countries that adopted Marxism-Leninism. Cuba and the Soviet Union made several economic deals with each other.

Castro feared the US would sponsor a coup to overthrow him due to his ties with the communist Soviet Union and his disdain for America. To deter this, he created the People's Militia, which consisted of fifty thousand Cuban civilians. He even received support from some US citizens when he made a visit to the United Nations in New York City.

His supporters shouted slogans to show their support for him and what Cuba was doing. "Cuba is not for sale!" "Down with Yankee imperialism!" The crowd was loud, but although they threw pennies, the protest did not turn violent.

During his visit, Castro met with anti-establishment figures like Malcolm X. Castro's speech to the United Nations Assembly lasted more than four and a half hours. He bashed the United States for its capitalist policies that affected Latin America.

The Bay of Pigs Invasion

In 1961, the US Embassy in Havana suffered a crippling blow, as much of its staff was expelled. Castro believed there were spies working there. The United States retaliated by formally cutting ties with Cuba. Before Eisenhower left office, the CIA was in the beginning stages of planning a coup to overthrow the Castro regime.

In 1960, Eisenhower gave the green light for the CIA to carry out the plan. CIA agents arrived in Guatemala to begin training. By November, a small unit known as the Cuban Democratic Revolutionary Front had been trained in guerilla warfare.

Another group that was formed the following year was the Cuban Revolutionary Council, which was led by José Miró Cardona. Prior to leaving the country, he had served as prime minister. Castro took over after he left. (Cardona was not pushed out by Castro; it seems Cardona could see the writing on the wall of what was to come under a regime heavily influenced by Castro.) If Cardona was successful in his efforts to overthrow Castro, the US agreed he should become the president until elections could be held.

The plan to overthrow Cuba was supposed to be kept quiet. However, exiled Cubans in Miami were made aware of the plans, and it became a topic of frequent conversation. Unbeknownst to the United States government, spies for Castro had already situated themselves in Florida and learned of the planned invasion.

The plans for the operation were taken up by John F. Kennedy, who was inaugurated as president in 1961. The following April, the US-led invasion of Cuba began. One small group of Cuban exile forces would be deployed to the eastern coast of Cuba to distract Castro from the Bay of Pigs.

At the outset, the US intended to launch airstrikes on two of Cuba's air bases. More than 1,400 Cuban exiles arrived in a surprise attack while paratroopers attempted to disrupt the advancement of Cuban forces.

Meanwhile, members of the United Revolutionary Front would have people on standby in South Florida, awaiting word of the invasion. If the invasion was a success, they would be sent to Cuba to help form a provisional government.

On April 15th, 1961, eight bombers left Nicaragua to carry out the airstrike. The CIA used B-26 bombers and disguised them as planes belonging to the Cuban Air Force. However, the bombers were outdated and failed to hit their intended targets. Kennedy canceled the second airstrike.

Two days later, a brigade landed at the Bay of Pigs, only to be met by Cuban forces. The Cuban Air Force sank ships and disrupted the advances of the Cuban exiles on the ground. Half of the exile-backed air support was destroyed due to the Cubans' overwhelmingly larger force. Castro dispatched twenty thousand troops, which greatly outnumbered the Bay of Pigs invasion forces, and the Cuban Air Force remained on high alert well into the next day. On April 19th, President Kennedy ordered an air operation to protect the remaining B-26 bombers.

The Cuban forces destroyed them. As a result, the planned invasion failed. While some of the exiles escaped, many of them were either imprisoned or executed for their efforts.

The failed Bay of Pigs invasion became a blemish on President John F. Kennedy's legacy. However, it would not be the last time he dealt with a situation in Cuba during his short time in office.

Cuban Missile Crisis

In 1962, the Soviet Union sought to strengthen its military might. Soviet Premier Nikita Khrushchev wished to install nuclear missiles on Cuban soil. Castro accepted the offer, confident that Cuba would be protected by the Soviet Union from a possible US invasion while further galvanizing Marxist-Leninist ideology (Castro admitted he was a Marxist-Leninist at the end of 1961).

The United States discovered the Soviet missiles by way of aircraft recon photos. The discovery led to the Cuban Missile Crisis. Castro claimed the missiles were there for defense purposes, but the United States believed the Soviets would use Cuba to launch offensive attacks.

In response, Kennedy sent American naval units to create a blockade. He made it clear the United States was ready to use military force if an attack was imminent. From October 16th to October 29th, countries around the world were on the edge of their seats, hoping a nuclear war didn't take place.

On October 27th, a US recon plane was in the process of heading back to Florida when it was shot down by a missile. The pilot, Rudolf Anderson, was killed, which only served to heighten tensions. Meanwhile, an invasion force was on standby in Florida.

The same day Anderson lost his life, the Soviet Union and the US were trying to reach some kind of compromise. Neither side wanted an all-out war to break out. Khrushchev sent a message to Kennedy stating that the missiles would be removed if the United States promised not to invade Cuba and if the United States removed its missiles from Turkey and southern Italy (some argue the missiles in southern Italy were not part of the deal; the agreement was rather secretive, so it is likely we will never know the full details).

In return, the Soviets removed their missiles from Cuba. Castro was intentionally left out of the negotiations and felt he had been betrayed by someone whom he saw as a worthy ally.

In the aftermath, Castro proposed the United States withdraw its forces from Guantanamo Bay Naval Base, which the US had held since 1903. It had been permanently leased to the US, which meant that it paid for the base each year (the US still pays Cuba for the naval base to this day, but Cuba refuses to cash the checks). The Cuban government believed the US had taken the land by force and wanted it back. Castro also asked the US to cease violating Cuba's marine territory and air space and to end its support for dissidents of the regime. The United States quickly disregarded his proposal.

In 2002, a military prison was opened at Guantanamo Bay. It has come under scrutiny for alleged cases of violating human rights. The US has no term limit on the lease to Guantanamo Bay, so its presence there will only end if it decides to leave or if some kind of agreement can be reached with Cuba.

Cuba in the 1960s and 1970s

Throughout the 1960s and 1970s, Cuba faced economic problems. In 1969, much of its sugar crops were destroyed by a hurricane, resulting in a challenging harvest. The country failed to meet the export quota. Castro felt as if he had failed his people and offered to resign.

However, the Cubans loved him. Yes, the economy was suffering, but Castro changed the way the peasants lived. Education was strong, and the people's healthcare was better than it had ever been. Most people had homes (Cuba provides housing to the people because housing is government-owned), and Castro constructed a vast network of roads in the country. Life could be difficult, but to most people, life was better than it had been under other rulers.

The Soviet Union offered to help Cuba sort out its economic problems. The economy witnessed growth in 1974 when sugar prices rose. In addition to this, several nations provided Cuba with credit. The economy would suffer again by 1980, as the sugar market once again declined.

When it came to international politics, Castro focused his attention on Angola, located in southwestern Africa. The country became embroiled in a civil war in 1975, and Castro threw his support behind the communist People's Movement for the Liberation of Angola (PMLA). In November 1975, Castro sent Cuban forces to Angola. The Soviet Union also sent troops. Their support ended in 1991 with the Soviet Union's dissolution, but the PMLA was ultimately successful.

The Mariel Boatlift and Renewed US Tensions

By the 1980s, Cuba was financially desperate, and the government sold valuable goods in exchange for US-made electronics via illegal trade channels in Panama. Over time, many Cubans left and sought refuge in Florida. Castro saw this as an opportunity to get rid of what he deemed were "undesirables." He sent away gay men, criminals, and the mentally ill.

More than 120,000 Cubans left Mariel, which is about twenty-five miles west of Havana, for Miami. The incident is known as the Mariel boatlift. When Ronald Reagan became president in 1981, he made it clear his administration would make plans to remove Castro from power.

Throughout the 1980s, Reagan kept tabs on Castro, which included aiding anti-communist forces in Central America, such as the Contras in their effort to defeat the Sandinistas. The US support of the Contras has been seen in a negative light, as the Contras utilized terror tactics and committed human rights violations.

In a journal entry dated to 1982, President Reagan noted that Jamaican Prime Minister Edward Seaga had beaten former Prime Minister Michael Manley in the 1980 election. Manley was backed by Castro and the Communist Party of Cuba. Reagan and Seaga sought to prevent the Caribbean from becoming a "red lake."

Cuba's attempts to spread communism would soon be known, and the United States found itself in the thick of it.

The Grenada Incident

Prior to 1974, Grenada was under the authority of the British Crown. Independence would not be easy for those in Grenada. Five years later, the New Jewel Movement led by Maurice Bishop seized power. Under the regime, political prisoners were incarcerated, and the constitution was suspended.

Throughout his tenure, Bishop modeled his leadership after Castro. He established ties with Cuba and the Soviet Union. One of the major projects he greenlit was the construction of an international airport. Reagan insisted the airport was actually a way to accommodate Soviet aircraft in the area.

By 1983, Grenada's party leadership had begun to break down. A group of military officers gave Bishop an ultimatum: share power with his deputy prime minister or resign from his post. Bishop refused and was eventually placed under arrest.

He was later freed during a demonstration put together by supporters. Bishop traveled to Fort Rupert (today's Fort George), where he was confronted by military forces. He was captured and then executed, along with other members of his Cabinet.

One of Bishop's murderers dismembered his body and burned it, along with the Cabinet members who were also killed. Their remains have never been found. After Bishop's death, Bernard Coard assumed power.

Around this time, the Grenadian military issued a curfew that threatened anyone with execution if they violated it. Soon, President Reagan began preparations for a United States-led invasion of Grenada.

During the invasion, which lasted from October 25th to October 29th, 1983, nearly eight hundred Cuban nationals were on the island. Many of them were construction workers (who also doubled as military reservists), but others worked in various occupations, including military roles.

US Special Forces were deployed to Grenada on October 23rd. Navy SEALs and the US Air Force were sent as well. Four SEALs were killed in a non-combat-related incident due to a failed helicopter drop. The SEALs attempted another mission the following day, but it was later canceled due to the weather.

All told, Reagan sent around two thousand United States military members to Grenada. They invaded the island on October 25th, using the very little intelligence they had. The US was soon confronted by Grenadian forces, along with the Cuban military, which was already on the island.

More troops from the United States, with assistance from the Organization of American States, would soon arrive, bringing the number of US troops up to seven thousand. The United States beat back the communist forces because of its overwhelming military might. The United States lost nineteen soldiers, while the Grenadians and Cubans lost a combined sixty-nine men.

Bernard Coard was arrested, along with others, due to their association with the murder of Maurice Bishop and several of his Cabinet members. Coard was originally sentenced to death, but his sentence was commuted to life imprisonment in 1991. As of this writing, he remains in prison.

The Grenada incident put Cuba on high alert. Castro even verbally attacked the Reagan administration, calling it fascist and warmongering.

Post-Soviet Cuba

In 1985, Mikhail Gorbachev took over as the premier of the Soviet Union. He launched a series of political and economic reforms known as *perestroika* and *glasnost.* Castro denounced these reforms and claimed they threatened the principles of socialism.

When the Soviet Union fell in 1991, the Cuban economy witnessed a large decline. The communist power had provided Cuba with annual financial assistance totaling billions of dollars. To Castro, it must have seemed as if socialism was on its last legs. The last of the Soviet troops left Cuba in September of 1991.

During Castro's last decade in power, he ensured that Marxist-Leninist ideology remained alive and well in Latin America. He threw his support behind leaders like Hugo Chávez in Venezuela. Castro would retire from his role as ruler of Cuba after nearly a half-century in power. His brother Raúl would take over in 2008.

US-Cuba relations were restored when Raúl Castro and US President Barack Obama made deals that expanded trade and travel. At home, Raúl began to decentralize and relax many economic policies that his brother had enacted.

By the time Obama left the presidency in 2017, he would repeal the Wet Foot, Dry Foot policy. When it was enacted in 1995, Cubans who had escaped and successfully landed on American soil were given the right to stay and receive United States citizenship.

When Donald Trump assumed the presidency, some of these policies were reversed, but the ties between the two countries remained intact.

Fidel Castro died at the age of ninety on November 25th, 2016. He left behind a controversial legacy. There are still Cubans and others around the world who admire him, but there are also many who resent what his regime did to the island nation of Cuba.

Final Thoughts

Fidel Castro put the United States on edge for many decades because of his association with the Soviet Union. The United States believed that communism was the greatest threat to freedom and would do anything to prevent its spread.

Thus, any presence of communism close to its shores was seen as an act of hostility. However, in the 21st century, tensions eased, and diplomatic ties between the two countries were normalized.

The future of Cuba and US relations seems promising, although there are some concerning reports. Cuba itself still remains a communist nation, so there will likely be the threat of tensions for decades to come. However, the threat of war is not high, especially when compared to the Cold War.

Chapter 10 – The Caribbean in the Late 20th Century to the Present Day

The Soviet Union collapsed in 1991, bringing an end to the threat of communism to the Caribbean. Cuba remained (and still remains) the only Marxist-Leninist nation in the Americas. And although Cuba suffered an economic decline, Castro remained resilient about ruling the country his way.

With the exception of Cuba, some Caribbean nations would have free elections for the first time in many years, as the threat of authoritarian dictatorships was no more. However, some nations continued to face unrest against the governments that were in power.

The rest of the Caribbean would enjoy peace and prosperity throughout the last decade of the 20th century and up until today when compared to the early 20th century. Its economy has been strengthened by trade and tourism. However, poverty and violence are still prevalent in most Caribbean countries today. This chapter will cover the last ten years of the 20th century and a bit about the present day.

Haiti in the Aristide Years and the Ongoing Conflict

For the first time since its inception in 1804, Haiti held its first democratic election in 1990. The leading candidate was Jean-Bertrand Aristide, who won the election and took office on February 7th, 1991. About eight months later, he was overthrown in a coup due to his progressive reforms and exiled.

His exile would last three years. Many Haitians residing in the United States supported Aristide and called on President Bill Clinton to play a role in bringing the deposed leader back to power in October 1994.

Aristide was reelected president in 2000. During his time in office, he called on France to pay $21 billion for the effects of French colonization and the events that took place between 1825 to 1947. Aristide faced rebels, who created violent conflicts in their efforts to remove the president from power.

In 2004, Aristide was exiled once again. This time, he would flee to South Africa, although he and others would claim that he had been kidnapped. What happened is still debated to this day, but Aristide claimed the US and France had something to do with his kidnapping. The South African government provided the deposed leader and his family with housing and staff. While there, he studied African languages at the University of South Africa.

Despite being in exile, he continued to criticize the ongoing politics in Haiti. The Lavalas (a political organization that supported Aristide) were targeted. Some were severely beaten, kidnapped, and/or killed.

As the years passed, people began to talk more and more about bringing Aristide back to Haiti. He finally returned to Haiti in 2011. After his return, he removed himself from the political world. But three years later, in September 2014, Aristide was placed under house arrest as part of a corruption investigation.

As of today, Aristide is no longer under house arrest. In 2021, he spent a month in Cuba for what was described as "medical treatment." He currently lives in Haiti while keeping a low profile from public life.

Aristide's legacy is remembered as positive. He helped pass several reforms that benefited the country, such as improving education and healthcare for Haiti's citizens. Aristide improved civil liberties and human rights. He also disbanded the paramilitary groups. (Remember the Tonton Macoute? They were still around, but Aristide and the Lavalas helped disband them.) Although Aristide has been accused of violating human rights when it came to stopping rebellions, most people think of him in a positive light, as he did much to bring Haiti into the future.

Earthquakes in Haiti

On January 12th, 2010, a 7.0 magnitude earthquake occurred near Leogane. Around three million people were affected, and the death toll was believed to range anywhere from 100,000 to 316,000.

Port-au-Prince and many cities nearby sustained massive damages. Due to the thousands of deaths, hospitals and morgues were overrun with dead Haitians. Many of them were buried in mass graves.

Close to 300,000 buildings were badly damaged to the point where it was just easiest to demolish them. Almost all of Leogane was destroyed. Many of the people slept in the streets, while others built shanty towns close to their destroyed homes.

The Dominican Republic made preparations to receive refugees along its border. Resources were sent to Haiti, but their deployment was slow.

Looting and violent skirmishes took place days after the earthquake subsided. Despite this, many Haitians were united by the tragedy and marched peacefully while securing the streets.

The United States utilized its military to send supplies to Haiti, as most of its water system was filled with waste. The recovery efforts continued throughout the 2010s. More than two million Haitians were still in need of aid in 2017. Another earthquake struck the country in 2021, this time recording 7.2 on the moment magnitude scale. It was slightly stronger than the 2010 earthquake, and more than two thousand people died as a result. Hundreds of thousands of people required assistance. Recovery efforts were hampered due to Tropical Depression Grace, and although Haiti has received some assistance, it still needs millions of dollars to get back on track.

The Haitians' trust in their government is low, partly due to the assassination of Jovenel Moïse on July 7th, 2021. It is believed his death was caused by his efforts to hamper the drug trade. Haiti has seen the rise of gangs, with its members outnumbering and outgunning the police force.

As of today, Haiti is still recovering from the two major earthquakes. It's unknown when the country will reach complete recovery. However, the country has high hopes for its future stability.

Security in the Caribbean

Throughout most of the 20th century, communist regimes, guerilla forces, and subversion from foreign powers were seen as security threats in the Caribbean, at least from the outside looking in. In the century's final decade, that focus changed.

The Caribbean began to focus on political stability and ending drug trafficking. The drug supply chain began in much of Latin America. Traffickers passed through the Caribbean en route to the United States.

Throughout the 1990s, the Summit of the Americas discussed the US and the Caribbean nations and their security strategy. It sought policies that would create a safer Caribbean without threatening the sovereignty of nations, including Cuba.

Restoration of US-Cuba Relations

The United States and Cuba suffered from poor relations beginning in the early 1960s. In 2009, US President Barack Obama hinted the relationship between the two countries would thaw after more than a half-century. Obama lifted travel restrictions and allowed Cuban Americans to send money to family members living in Cuba for the first time in decades.

On December 17th, 2014, Obama and Raúl Castro announced the two countries would restore their diplomatic relations. The United States reopened its embassy in Havana, and the following year, the United States removed Cuba from its list of states that sponsor terrorism.

Obama became the first sitting president in nearly a century to visit Cuba, doing so in 2016. He called upon the Cuban government to continue the liberalization of its political and economic policies.

Signs of improved relations began when US commercial jets provided flights to Cuba. The US government also repealed the Wet Foot, Dry Foot policy and lifted trade embargoes.

US President Donald Trump reinstated some restrictions that Obama had gotten rid of. In May 2022, President Joe Biden put some policies back in place, such as family remittance, the family reunification program, and travel measures. The ties between Cuba and the United States remain intact, despite concerns about the health and safety of diplomatic staff situated in the island nation.

Havana syndrome, as it has been dubbed, is a mysterious illness that causes dizziness and hearing loss. The first reported cases began in 2016, but the number of cases picked up the following year. Under Trump, the United States expelled Cuban diplomats from the country due to this mysterious illness, believing Cuba to be behind it. Cuba denounced the expulsion and accused the Trump administration of backtracking the normalization of ties. It is still not known what causes Havana syndrome, although foreign involvement has been ruled out of the majority of cases.

The Castro era ended when Raúl Castro left the presidency in 2018. He was replaced by Miguel Díaz-Canel, making him the first Cuban leader without the Castro name in almost sixty years.

Barbados Becomes a Republic

There are so many countries in the Caribbean that we, unfortunately, don't have the space to look at them all, but we will look at one more in-depth. Barbados was under the authority of the British Crown since its discovery in 1625, although it was officially colonized two years later. The country would soon become one of the major seats of authority in the British Caribbean.

Barbados's first referendum to become a republic was held in 2008 (one had been introduced in Parliament in 2000 but went nowhere). The referendum ran concurrently with the general election. However, the referendum vote was called off due to election security concerns. The referendum would not be revisited until seven years later when Prime Minister Freundel Stuart brought it up.

The Barbados Parliament attempted to pass a constitutional amendment to confirm its independence as a republic. While there was enough to meet a two-thirds majority in the Senate, the House of Assembly did not have the votes. It failed to pass the House. However, the third time proved to be a charm when Prime Minister Mia Mottley (the first woman to be prime minister of Barbados) announced that Barbados would become a republic by 2021.

On November 30th, 2021, Barbados abolished the monarchy and became a republic. Sandra Mason became the first president of the Republic of Barbados and received well wishes from the British royal family. Today, Barbados is a republic under the British Commonwealth.

Final Thoughts

Today, the Caribbean still has many challenges to overcome, such as political unrest in Haiti, Jamaica's high murder rate, and crime in Saint Kitts and Nevis. While the Caribbean is typically safe for tourists, the people living in most of the Caribbean countries would tell a different story. (If you are traveling to the Caribbean or anywhere else in the world, always make sure to check updated travel guidelines.)

Cuba and the United States created a new path forward to restoring diplomatic relations. Barbados became a republic and no longer had to answer to the British Crown.

With Barbados becoming an independent republic, the future of other Caribbean nations remains to be seen, especially in the wake of King Charles III's ascension to the British throne. Will other nations, such as Saint Kitts and Nevis and Jamaica, follow suit? Will Curaçao find itself declaring its full independence from the Dutch?

We cannot predict the future. Yet, it should not come as a surprise that Caribbean nations still under the control of European countries might seek their independence in the years to come.

Conclusion

The Caribbean's history is vast and rich. It is a shame we don't have the time to talk about the islands in more detail. We highly encourage you to read and discover more about the region; our sources at the end of the book will point you in the right direction.

The Caribbean has been seen as a source of wealth throughout history, whether it involved the lucrative sugar trade or its picture-perfect beaches. But we should not forget that before the Caribbean was discovered by Europeans, several groups of indigenous people called it home. The Taíno suffered greatly during colonization. Disease, famine, and many other factors played a role in their near extinction. Descendants of the Taíno are still around today. The Kalinago (Caribs) have their own territory in Dominica in the Lesser Antilles.

Spain was the first to establish dominance in the region. But other great powers, like France and England, would not be far behind. Even smaller European nations like Denmark and Sweden briefly occupied parts of the Caribbean.

Over the years, the Caribbean witnessed economic prosperity in the colonies. Yet, it was built on the slave trade. Slaves faced violence, torture, and even death while working under the worst possible conditions. Slaves and freed slaves seized opportunities to revolt against the white colonists. Most revolts failed, but others were successful. One even led to independence.

When the United States became a more powerful nation, it set its sights on the Caribbean. It enacted policies to prevent foreign invasions while justifying its own actions in the Americas. Today, the United States retains the territories of Puerto Rico and the US Virgin Islands.

Due to its proximity and power, the United States featured heavily in 19th- and 20th-century Caribbean history (and likely will through the 21st century as well). It would gain both allies and adversaries in the region. For instance, when the potential danger of communism knocked on its back door with the ascension of Fidel Castro in Cuba, the US took notice and intervened.

So far, the 21st century has witnessed more nations becoming independent of European powers, and it seems likely this will continue throughout the century. While the Caribbean faces its fair share of problems today, it welcomes tourists from around the world to its idyllic white-sand beaches and crystal-clear waters. It is not known what the future holds for the Caribbean, but history tells us that we should pay attention, for history will likely be in the making as the years pass.

Part 2: The Golden Age of Piracy

A Captivating Guide to the Role of Pirates in Maritime History during the Early Modern Period, Including Stories of Anne Bonny, Sir Francis Drake, and William Kidd

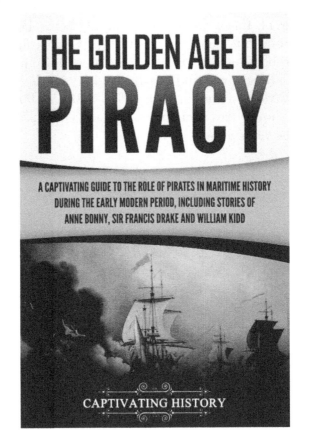

Introduction

The open sea. Waves splash about the ship's underside while the light wind fills the sails, pushing the vessel ever forward. There are a few seagulls in the sky and maybe a shark or two in the waters below, yet your ship remains stable. In a few short days, it will make it to one of the islands in the Caribbean, where you can transfer your precious cargo and receive payment for your troubles. You had to endure months of non-stop sailing, the hot and humid days followed by cold and ruthless nights, rotten food and moldy drinking water, the stench of your fellow sailors, and the poor reliability of the chart in front of you. But you will soon make it. Patience is all you need.

Suddenly, you spot a ship. At first, it raises the same flag that you have on your mainmast. It could be the Union Jack or the complex Merchant Flag of the Kingdom of France. It matters little because as soon as it approaches, the flag is struck, and a new one is raised— one that's all black. Or maybe it is black with a skull emblazoned on it, or perhaps there is a cutlass, or both, or neither. All in all, you know what you're in for, especially when the ship fires a single shot from one of its dozen or so guns. You have no choice—you must strike your flag and allow the people from the other vessel to board yours.

And board it, they do. Most of them are young men, filthy and smelly from days spent on the open sea (much like yourself and your crew), and most of them are armed with a single pistol and a single blade. Their outfits are simple and practical, and most of them look the same, except for one. The one distinctly dressed like a gentleman approaches you, maybe with a grin, maybe with a stern expression, and starts discussing terms. Your vessel seems fine enough, and the cargo you carry might be to their interest, though not all of it. You're left with some provisions and maybe some money to make it back safely (or to save face with your employers), but everything else now belongs to this man and his crew, right down to your ship. He tells you not to worry, that you will take their ship, which looks damaged and leaky all over. Then he inspects your crew. Your surgeon and your navigator are the first men he singles out, and with a barely veiled threat, he lets them know that they are now switching crews. He extends this proposal to others on board, and quite a few of your own men decide to join him, be it out of cowardice, disrespect to you, or a simple desire to survive (or share the spoils of the loot they spent months transporting across the ocean aboard your ship). Once everything is done, you and what's left of your crew move to the other ship.

You're safe and sound, but your cargo, as well as your crew, has been carved until there was nothing left. You know that your superiors will care little about this encounter, and you know that you will either have to recoup the costs or spend some time in a dungeon as punishment. At best, you can lose your job and hope for someone to hire you. It's a world that's far from fair, and you wonder why you didn't join the crew that just left you destitute and in a rickety old sloop that looks like it might fall apart at the slightest wind. In the distance, you can hear the music aboard your former ship; the men who stole it from you are celebrating, probably on their way to waste your cargo on refitting that same ship but more likely on liquor, food, and loose women.

Yes, this yarn sounds familiar, as it should, for tales of pirates often sound alike. The exciting part comes from one important fact—everything that was just described was an everyday occurrence for the better part of both the 17th and 18th centuries, and it spanned at least five continents and included tens of thousands of people, both at sea and on land.

Piracy is not a new phenomenon. Indeed, it has existed ever since early man figured out that he could trade goods via rivers, lakes, seas, and oceans. And with seaborne trade being more active now than ever before in human history, piracy will not be going away any time soon. However, there was a time, not that long ago, when piracy was more than just a passing problem that interfered with trade. Indeed, it was possibly the most serious issue that nations had to face back then, an issue that could literally halt trade and whose impact could affect events in history. It was a time when pirates could be the direct result of countries losing wars, armies losing men, and ordinary people losing sleep. It was a time when ordinary men could earn immense wealth through illicit means, of course, and where that little bit of freedom came with the highest price imaginable: death. A time that did not include a lot of eyepatches, buried treasure, or swashbuckling charismatic heroes but did include brutal executions, impressive raids, and even a few self-made kings along the way. Historians aptly call this period the Golden Age of Piracy, and it was the one time where the so-called sweet trade could flourish almost unchallenged.

In this tome, we will cover the history of the Golden Age, focusing on factual information and dispelling a few myths along the way. Some readers might be disappointed to learn that some of the most prevailing "facts" about pirates from history are not facts at all but mere fabrications by contemporary authors or modern popular culture. However, the real stories behind the myths and fables are far more fascinating, and they present a notable chapter of world history in every sense of the word. You're about to embark upon a globetrotting adventure of wealth and poverty, excitement and danger, booze and blood, life and death. In short, the history of the Golden Age of Piracy is one that's more than deserving of extensive historical coverage, and you're going to find out why in the chapters to come.

Model of Blackbeard's original pirate ship Queen Anne's Revenge

Chapter 1 – Brief History of Piracy: Defining the Terminology, Early Historical Accounts of Maritime Crime, Outlining the Golden Age

Defining the Term "Pirate"

Most people have a vague idea of what a pirate is, and if we were to break it down in the simplest terms, the definition would be "an individual who attacks and robs ships at sea." However, this definition is not particularly helpful since it omits more than a few details. The most important detail is who the attacker is. Sir Francis Drake, for example, would routinely attack and rob ships at sea, but if you were his fellow English citizen and you were to call him a pirate back in the day, he would be offended. Of course, if you were Spanish, i.e., Drake's enemy in combat, and used the same term to describe him, he wouldn't much care. As an aside, Drake was a prominent privateer who died in 1596, half a century before the beginning of what we call the Golden Age of Piracy. Though he perfectly fits the personalities and experiences of many pirates described in this tome, he was active long before any of them were even born.

Over the years, the sea brigands were referred to by various names interchangeably. Terms like "corsair," "buccaneer," "privateer," and others were bandied around as synonyms to the term "pirate." However, they are not the same. The confusion becomes even bigger when the terms overlap, as certain people involved with maritime activities would essentially shift from, for instance, being a privateer to being a pirate and vice versa.

With that in mind, it is instrumental to define these terms as best as possible. "Pirate" is a universal term for any type of crime that involves a huge body of water and a boat of any size. In other words, you can have sea pirates, lake pirates, river pirates, etc. Furthermore, the crimes don't even have to happen at sea. If you were a shipowner or a crew member, and you were committing crimes on land (looting, robbery, rape, murder, gambling, smuggling, etc.), you were a pirate. The word itself is Greek in origin, read as πειρατής (*peiratés*) and meaning "brigand."

So, what about the other terms? Let's start with "corsair." The term itself is French, originally written as *corsaire*, and it draws its roots from the Latin word *cursus*, meaning hostile attack or plunder. In other words, it draws roots from an illegal act, so it's linked to piracy, at least to some extent. However, the French did not use the term "corsair" for illegal activities when related to their own seamen. In fact, the term was specifically related to privateers from the small harbor town of Saint-Malo in the northwestern region of Brittany. Over time, Europeans would also refer to Muslim privateers from the African Barbary Coast as "Barbary corsairs" or "Turkish corsairs," though, in reality, these seafaring folks from Africa would not always be privateers. Sometimes, they were legitimate naval commanders from the Ottoman Empire; other times, they would be regional lords and outlaws, thus making them outright pirates. Furthermore, they were not all Berbers (a term used for the African native groups living in what is today Morocco, Algeria, and Tunisia). Since the Ottoman-commissioned Barbary corsairs would often attack Christian ships and wage war against the Christian soldiers, the term "corsair" also gained a bit of a religious undertone.

When we break it down, corsairs are effectively privateers. But what is a privateer? As its name suggests, it refers to a private vessel not owned by the state or the monarch. The term also refers to the officer in charge of the ship. To put it simply, both Sir Francis Drake and his vessel, *Golden Hind*, are privateers.

A privateer would work outside of the navy as a free agent mainly because there was no real royal navy among any of the seafaring empires during the Late Middle Ages. His job (more than 99 percent of privateers were men at the time) was usually to plunder and attack ships that belonged to nations against which his country was warring. For example, Amaro Pargo, a Spanish corsair/privateer, made a name for himself by attacking mostly English and Dutch ships. Richard Hawkins, one of Drake's men, also became famous for attacking ships that belonged to the Spanish Armada. But the activity of a privateer was not limited to warfare. In fact, it was expected they would go after merchant ships and other vessels that carried precious cargo. Not only would it provide rich plunder for them and their monarch, but it would also significantly cripple the economic well-being of a rival country. For that reason, a privateer of one country would be a notorious pirate of another. Both Oruç Reis (known as Oruç Barbarossa in Europe due to his ginger beard) and his brother Hayreddin (a later Ottoman navy admiral and *beylerbey*—"chief governor"—of Ottoman North Africa) were known as fierce pirates among the Western European sailors but were hailed as heroes and loyal subjects in the Ottoman Empire.

Of course, each privateer would be granted full permission from their monarch to plunder ships; these written permissions are called letters of marque, and every Western Christian nation, from Spain, Portugal, and France to England and the Netherlands, issued these permissions. Naturally, the permissions would be null and void the very second the two countries made peace, as doing so was seen as an act of goodwill and a step toward smooth peace negotiations. An immediate annulment of a letter of marque would leave privateers unsatisfied, which is, in fact, one of many contributors to the rise in piracy during the several decades that comprise the Golden Age.

While privateers had permission by the state to do whatever they wanted to an enemy ship, their actions were really no different from those of a common pirate. They would frequently be just as monstrous and brutal as some of the worst outlaws in maritime history. For these reasons and more, people, even back then, would consider privateering nothing more than state-sanctioned piracy. The letter of marque was really the only thing separating a privateer from a life of outright piracy, hence why such a document was incredibly important, legally speaking. Owning a letter of marque could get privateers a lenient sentence in case they went over the line.

Unlike corsairs, privateers were not always religiously motivated, although religion did play a huge part in their activities. For example, most of the privateers would prey on ships from nations with a completely different theological background. England and the Netherlands, two heavily Protestant countries, would wage war with Spain and Portugal, whose majority of people were staunch Catholics. But to a privateer, the target ship merely had to come from a nation with which their homeland was at war. In other words, if England and the Netherlands were skirmishing, Dutch ships would become fair game to privateers and vice versa.

Finally, there's the term "buccaneer" to consider. If corsairs were linked to the Mediterranean Sea and privateers to the Protestant nations of the Atlantic and Western Europe, buccaneers found their place in the Caribbean, more specifically in the islands of Hispaniola (divided into the Dominican Republic and Haiti today) and Tortuga (just north of Haiti). The name itself derives from the French (or rather Caribbean Arawak) word "buccan." A buccan was a type of wooden framework that hunters would use to either slow-roast or smoke meat. Interestingly, buccaneers were originally nothing more than French-born hunters who settled in Hispaniola and made their living from hunting wild game.

With the Spanish efforts to cleanse most of their West Indies' territories from French interlopers, the early buccaneers moved to Tortuga, a far smaller isle than Hispaniola with fewer natural resources. This course of events pushed them further into piracy, and soon enough, they would be attacking Spanish galleons with alarming frequency, prompting other nations such as the Dutch and the English to provide them with letters of marque and employ them as privateers. Some of the biggest names among the buccaneers, including Daniel Montbars and François L'Olonnais, would be active during the very early days of the Golden Age of Piracy. While they are often counted among some of the most famed pirates of their time, they were effectively privateers or regular seafarers (or not even seafarers at all) who were pushed into effective piracy by the Spanish.

As you can see, there are so many overlapping themes that we can almost forgive people for conflating all of these terms. And to make matters worse, it is sometimes incredibly difficult to pin down what these men exactly were, despite how other contemporary people described them or even despite how these men described themselves. The famous (or rather infamous) Captain William Kidd, as we will see later in this volume, vehemently denied that he was a pirate, constantly proclaiming that he was hired as a buccaneer, which was not false. However, he did commit acts (or rather, some acts were attributed to him) that would undeniably be linked to piratical activity. In addition, former pirates like Benjamin Hornigold would turn to become pirate hunters, privateers, or regular merchants with a proper pardon from the monarch. Therefore, legally speaking, they would not be referred to as pirates, at least not until they broke the conditions of their pardons and struck a merchant ship again. In addition, false accusations of piracy were common during those years, especially among seamen who felt unsatisfied with the conditions on their ships or who simply felt mutinous for one reason or another. Despite all of that confusion regarding terminology, the undeniable fact remains that pirates did, indeed, exist, and their exploits are just as complicated as anything else in society can be.

A Brief History of Piracy

Most of the terms related to piracy that we've listed above stem from either the Middle Ages or modern times. However, the very act of piracy itself is quite old. To put it in the simplest terms possible, maritime crime is as old as seafaring itself. In antiquity, Tyrrhenians, Phoenicians, and Illyrians all frequently dabbled in piracy, while in ancient Greece, it was considered a legal and morally justified venture (though this changed in later years). In fact, a rather famous anecdote from antiquity regarding pirates involves none other than the most famous Roman ruler ever, Gaius Julius

Caesar. On his voyage across the Aegean Sea, the former priest-turned-military commander Caesar was captured by a group of Cilician pirates. They reportedly ransomed him for a sum of twenty talents of silver. For reference, one talent roughly corresponds to thirty-three kilograms of raw metal, so in today's currency, that would be around $25,040 per talent, making the ransom $500,080. Caesar, however, felt insulted by this ransom, demanding that they raise it to fifty talents, or $1,252,000 in today's money. During Caesar's captivity at the island of Pharmacusa (modern-day Pharmakonisi), a small section of the Dodecanese Islands off the coast of modern-day Turkey, he promised that he would crucify each and every one of his pirate captors, which they took as a joke. As soon as his ransom was paid and he was back in Rome, Caesar raised a massive fleet, hunted down his former captors, and captured them. True to his word, he crucified them all, but he did show a bit of leniency by having their throats cut so they could die quickly.

The Early Middle Ages also saw lots of pirate activity. Vikings of Scandinavia were constantly raiding the European coast with plenty of success, and their seafaring warriors would frequently go after the British Isles as well, which even led to early Scandinavian settlements in what would later become England. Off the coast of modern-day Netherlands, the Frisian sea brigands would often attack the Holy Roman Empire's ships, with the most prominent commanders being Pier Gerlofs Donia and Wijerd Jelckama. The south Mediterranean coast of Europe was under constant assault by the so-called Moorish pirates, while the Slavic tribe known as the Narentines would frequently raid the Adriatic coast. People across Europe had their own brand of pirate attackers to worry about, and brigands would vary in nationality, culture, and efficacy. Anyone, from the Baltic Slavs and Cossacks to the Arabians and Greek Maniots, could be atop a ship's deck and raiding the nearest seaborne merchant vessel. And while there were exceptions to the rule in every century of European history, pirates were considered a threat to society and criminals who deserved brutal punishment.

Of course, piracy is by no means limited to Europe. In fact, entire armadas of pirates could be found in ancient and medieval China, Japan, Vietnam, and the many Indian states. There were even pirates off both the east and west coasts of Africa. In fact, many of these ships would actually come across European vessels, and depending on the relations between the countries, there would either be plundering or a peaceful departure. In fact, if a piratical act were to take place between, for example, the English and the Mughal Empire of India, it would amount to a political scandal, and we intend to cover one such event later in this book. Every single navigable ocean has seen its fair share of piracy throughout the entirety of human history, and each culture would have differing views on piracy as a phenomenon. As you will see later, despite the act being highly illegal and condemned by society, there were even contemporary citizens that found the lifestyle fascinating. Millions of people would willingly abandon their regular lives and sail the seven seas looking for plunder.

Norsemen invading England, detail from Folio 9v of Miscellany on the Life of St. Edmund, published on January 1ˢᵗ, 1130, The Morgan Library & Museum, New York, NY, USA

https://commons.wikimedia.org/wiki/File:Miscellany_on_the_Life_of_St._Edmund_-_MS_M.736_fol._9v.jpg

Outlining the Golden Age of Piracy

Defining what exactly the Golden Age of Piracy was can be a bit daunting, especially considering the whole issue of defining the terms such as "pirate" or "privateer." Most experts would agree that there were roughly three periods that marked the so-called Golden Age, and they use several different factors when considering this issue. Firstly, in order for a time span to be the golden age of anything, there has to be an increase in frequency. Next, there has to be an exact cut-away point, i.e., a point in time where a certain activity starts to significantly wane or stop altogether. Finally, a golden age has to show certain trends in society, trends that would set the stage for the golden age to take place and thrive.

In relation to piracy itself, there are a few issue-specific factors to consider. Firstly, a golden age of piracy has to have prominent personalities that marked the age, so much so that they became the very stuff of legends. Next, for pirates to thrive, they need safe ports and places to congregate, i.e., semi-permanent or permanent pirate settlements. Lastly, the extent of piracy has to be so significant that it actually leads to changes in legal proceedings and gain attention from the very top of the state.

When we take every single factor listed above into consideration, we can more or less connect the dots and draw a concrete timeline of the Golden Age of Piracy. Most experts (though not all) would divide the Golden Age into three separate time periods, all perfectly leading one into the other. Those three would be:

- The buccaneering period (roughly between the early 1650s and 1680)

- The Pirate Round period (throughout the 1690s)

- The period immediately following the War of the Spanish Succession (between 1715 and 1726)

Before we move on, we should address a few discrepancies. Namely, despite the fact that the Golden Age, as outlined above, lasted around seventy-five or more years, it is by no means the only period with massive surges and resurgences in piracy. Piratical activities in the Mediterranean and in Southeast and East Asia were well underway for centuries before the buccaneers took up arms against the Spanish. On top of this, the piratical attacks did not necessarily decrease after the deaths of the most prominent pirates of the Caribbean in the late 1720s. In fact, some of the fiercest pirates in the world actually rose to prominence an entire century later, including one of the most successful female pirates to date, a former Chinese prostitute and pirate leader named Zheng Yi Sao. However, that topic is widely outside of the scope of this book.

Furthermore, these facts don't take away from the historical and cultural importance of the Golden Age of Piracy. It would, indeed, be this particular period that would push the pirates into the global mainstream, and some of the most prominent images we have of pirates today, complete with misconceptions and false attributions, will come from this exact timespan. Events in this particular age would directly influence the creation and standardization of national navies and the improvement of conditions of a common sailor. As odd as it might seem, the pirates that operated during these three-fourths of a century had a far more profound influence on the world than historians and everyday people give them credit for.

Chapter 2 – Prelude to the Golden Age: Events in Europe, Early Pirate Bases

Events in Europe Prior to the Golden Age of Piracy

In the early 17th century and beyond, Europe was a colossal battlefield due to a series of skirmishes known collectively as the European wars of religion. Nearly every single major European power was involved, including England, France, the Netherlands, Spain, Portugal, the Holy Roman Empire, the Italian lands, and the Scandinavian kingdoms. While religion was one of the main motivators behind these conflicts, with the rise of Protestant factions in Christianity and the waning Catholic influence over much of Western Europe, they were far from the only factor. Oftentimes, two Catholic or Protestant nations would clash against one another while allied with a country that would be deemed an enemy. Some of the bloodiest wars took place during these times, including the Thirty Years' War within the Holy Roman Empire (1618-1648), The Eighty Years' War, also known as the Dutch War of Independence (1568-1648), and the War of the Three Kingdoms that involved England, Scotland, and Ireland (1639-1651). Moreover, the wars in England would directly lead to Oliver

Cromwell overthrowing the king and establishing himself as Lord Protector of the Realm, effectively making England a republic for the first and, so far, final time in its existence.

Also, during this turbulent period, European maritime forces started colonizing other corners of the globe, creating new trade routes and importing brand-new products and raw materials. The English East India Company was still in its infancy, and both the French and the Portuguese were already active in the Indian Ocean. Of course, the future colonizers also sought good fortune across the Atlantic, with both Americas seeing a lot of activity.

The most prominent scrambles for supremacy in the region, however, happened in the so-called West Indies or the Caribbean. The many islands that comprise the region would serve as bases for several great European powers, with Spain holding sway until the waning years of the 17ᵗʰ century. Many seafarers of French, Dutch, and English origin found their calling here either as plantation owners, hunters, sailors, or outright pirates. As the decades went by, more and more territories were ceded from Spain to the other European powers. For instance, Jamaica was held by the Spanish until 1655, when Admiral William Penn conquered it and subjugated it to English rule. In addition, the western part of Hispaniola was Spanish, though the French managed to establish a settlement there in 1670, with the western half of the island officially being ceded to France nine years later. This region would eventually become Haiti.

The ethnic makeup of these islands was interesting, to say the least. Each island had its own native population of various people groups, and interbreeding with Europeans was common at the time. However, most invading powers also imported thousands of slaves from Africa to the region, therefore further diluting the native population. Because of so many various people groups essentially being forced to work side by side with one another on a daily basis, they had to find a way to interact, which led to the creation of early Creole languages.

Interestingly, the trade route from the Caribbean to Europe was not the busiest, as most Europeans still frequently traded with East Asia and the Indian subcontinent. The powerful Mughal Empire was still the dominant force, both on land and at sea, having reached its peak during the reigns of two rulers known as the Great Moghuls colloquially—Emperor Shah Jahan (r. 1628-1658) and especially Emperor Aurangzeb (r. 1658-1707). The empire's influence was so vast that it could wipe out any of the European trading companies in an instant. The English East India Company, in particular, was essentially forced into keeping good relations with the empire, considering they only had a few factories on the subcontinent at the time. More importantly, the region was known for its spices and other materials, of which the European elites were incredibly fond. Foreign ships had to maintain their strenuous relationships with the Mughal Empire as best as they knew how, and that meant preventing any piratical activity from targeting Indian merchant ships. With the wars in Europe draining the court treasuries and the colonies growing increasingly restless, violent, and—most importantly—lawless, the seeds were sown for the first prominent pirates to emerge.

Early Pirate Bases

One common myth, which we will delve into deeper a bit later, was that the pirates during the Golden Age were so prominent that they essentially established a "Pirate Republic," which was free from all European powers and responsible only to itself and its maritime citizens. However, nothing can be further from the truth. Throughout the Golden Age, there was no such thing as a pirate utopia. However, pirates did often congregate in specific areas, be they small islands or port towns. Unsurprisingly, they were all prominent spots on major trade routes, and even less surprisingly, they were all spots where illegal trade was allowed and where officials turned a blind eye to contraband retail.

Before we move onto the prominent pirate bases themselves, we should discuss the legal activities of maritime empires at the time. It is no secret that the law had little to no effect in certain corners of huge seafaring empires. However, the laws regarding trade were not that different from our own in the 21st century. For example, if a person came into possession of a huge sum of wealth overnight, the matter would be investigated thoroughly. Seafarers, in particular, were subject to these investigations, considering the prominence of piracy and the insecurity of contemporary ocean trade. Moreover, if pirates from one country attacked ships that belonged to an ally nation, the matter would become an international incident, and unless the native authorities dealt with the issue, the matter could easily lead to war.

These matters became exceptionally difficult during times when peace treaties were signed between two nations. Back in the day, news traveled slow, especially across the ocean. So, if, for instance, Spain and England signed a treaty that demanded an end to all hostilities, privateers on either side would have to cease attacking ships from their former enemies. Since said news would sometimes take months to reach people outside of Europe, a privateer could easily attack a ship, thinking they were doing so fully protected by the law. In reality, though, the attack would be considered an act of aggression and a breach of the treaty, resulting in another potential war or monetary compensation. It was a vicious circle and a legal nightmare for everyone involved.

Of course, these factors were not the only ones that played a major role in forming regular pirate bases. In fact, everyday seafaring might have been far more influential in that regard. Generally speaking, if you were a sailor in the mid- to late 17th century and early 18th century, no matter what country you were living in, you would be living a miserable life. Average wages of common sailors were incredibly low, and most people who held high positions, such as admirals or captains, didn't fare much better during a typical nautical voyage. More importantly, as a sailor, your chances of advancing to a ranked position were almost impossible. You would essentially be risking life and limb to import some fabric, spices, wood, and other raw materials, and those risks would seemingly come from everywhere. You might die from malnutrition, drown at sea due to a storm, be killed by locals in any number of non-European ports, get stranded somewhere for even the slightest insubordination, contract and succumb to one of countless diseases, be murdered by the local wildlife, end up being sold into slavery if you had the misfortune of being attacked by a slave-selling nation, and, of course, be killed by pirates. And to make matters worse, you would be at the mercy of your commanding officer, and your amenities were practically non-existent. The job essentially trapped you into a life of utter misery.

Compared to these conditions, the life of piracy was almost seen as a blessing, although working aboard a pirate ship was no better than being on an ordinary vessel in terms of simple living and working conditions. Many young men turned to piracy for the same reason they would become factory workers in the ever-growing East India Company—it was a position that would, at the very least, offer them new wealth and a chance to be, to a certain extent, their own bosses. The main difference, of course, was the social attitude toward the men who chose these career paths. East India Company employees, be they ordinary workers, factors (mercantile fiduciaries of the EIC), writers, etc., were usually disliked by the English upper classes, but their work was not illegal or even particularly unethical for the time. Piracy, on the other hand, was an out-and-out crime, and few men actually confessed to being pirates openly. In fact, the punishments for acts of piracy were severe, usually consisting of hanging, beheading, being drawn and quartered, or a combination of these acts. Furthermore, a pirate's body would usually be coated in tar or hung in chains above a prominent port as a reminder to other seafarers what awaited them if they turned to piracy. Despite all of that, thousands of men, usually those in their twenties, would opt to sail under the black flag and, if necessary, die under it.

An average successful pirate ship could haul in massive booty. And considering their targets were usually massive galleons that transported tons of goods and valuables, a typical pirate could earn himself a wage that was hundreds of times larger than a regular sailor's daily salary. Naturally, a pirate ship would need a safe place to deposit all of the riches stolen from a ship, mainly because the authorities would certainly get suspicious if a small, ill-fit vessel entered a harbor and its sailors, all poorly dressed and lacking in basic manners, were in possession of exotic goods worth tens of thousands of pounds. Not only would pirates need a port at which to resell all of their stolen goods quickly, but they also required an area where they might rest, eat, drink, enjoy a woman or two, and repair their ships. Such ports already existed in the Mediterranean, with the Barbary Corsairs using them prominently, but as the decades progressed, a few new key areas arose as potential pirate bases, one of which would serve as the potential inspiration for a fictional pirate utopia.

One of these ports was Tortuga, a small island north of Hispaniola. Originally settled by the Spanish in 1625, it would be the home base of French buccaneers, as well as both English and Dutch pirates, for many decades, with the Spanish retaking and losing the island several times. By 1640, the French eventually built a permanent fortress on the island called Fort de Rocher, allowing them to fend off Spanish attacks in the coming years. And even as the piratical activity moved to different islands in the region, some of the most famed pirates of the time, including Henry Morgan, frequented Tortuga. Morgan would be an instrumental member of the so-called Brethren of the Coast, a very loosely connected group of seafaring outlaws mostly of French Huguenot and British Protestant descent. This brotherhood was, to an extent, responsible for making the Caribbean an economic hub thanks to their illegal trade, and many of the pirates would try to retire on the islands as farmers or plantation owners with varying success.

West of the Caribbean, within Mexico, we find another early pirate base, the town of Campeche. Originally a trading town formed in the 1540s, the place would become a hotbed of piracy, with the Spanish government unable to quench the problem for at least a century and a half. Sir Francis Drake was one of the first privateers to sail the waters near Campeche, but the city itself would host, in one way or another, a vast array of famous pirates, buccaneers, privateers, and other men of the sea. Possibly the most famed men to be in or near the city were the brutal French buccaneer Jean David Nau (better known as François L'Olonnais), Dutch mercenary and pirate Laurens de Graaf, and the renowned Welsh pirate and later lieutenant governor of Jamaica, Sir Henry Morgan. In fact, Morgan would be one of many seafaring bandits that would sack Campeche and rob it of its riches.

Staying within the Caribbean, we move onto possibly the most famous bases for any pirate during the Golden Age, namely Nassau on the island of New Providence (the Bahamas) and Port Royal in Jamaica. Port Royal was inhabited as early as 1494 by the Spanish, but it officially became an English territory in 1655 after a successful invasion. Around the same time, the Bahamas were being settled, with New Providence getting its first settlement in 1666. Charles Town, the fort (and later the town), was founded in 1670 and served as a privateering base for the British, who renamed it Nassau in 1695, a year after it was raided by the Spanish. Both Nassau and Port Royal were infamous pirate dens even during their early days, with contemporary reports mentioning drunkards, illegal traders, prostitutes, and general lawlessness. The situation would improve slightly in the early years of the 18th century when the local governors and other officials started to crack down on piracy, with business slowly turning to slavery, plantation maintenance, legal trade, and other venues.

Interestingly, no less than three early pirate bases were founded thousands of miles away from the Caribbean off the southeastern coast of Africa—more specifically, on the island of Madagascar. The northeastern part of the island housed two such bases, those being Ranter Bay (modern-day Rantabe) and the island of Île Sainte-Marie, while the third base, the former Fort Dauphin (modern-day Tôlanaro), was located in the southeast. Madagascar's pirate bases were strategically located thanks to the continuous trade between the Europeans and the South and Southeast Asians. All sea routes had to go around the south of Africa, and aside from Madagascar, there were few landmasses within the Indian Ocean where traders could dock their ships. Furthermore, ships from the Middle East and the Mughal Empire would often trade in the waters of the Red Sea, which was right between Africa and Asia and north of Madagascar. These routes proved to be a wealthy source of potential booty for pirates, and indeed more than a few famous pirate raids took place in these waters.

However, Madagascar is also important in pirate lore for a different set of reasons. Namely, despite not having its own Brethren of the Coast like the Caribbean, it did house a few territories that would inspire the existence of the so-called Libertatia, or the Republic of Pirates. As we will see, some of the pirates who made their stay on Madagascar did go on to influence the local people into engaging in skirmishes and even full-on wars, with a few of the seafarers even going as far as to declare themselves kings. However, these events did not last long, and the influence of piracy more or less waned on the island within a few decades after the Golden Age.

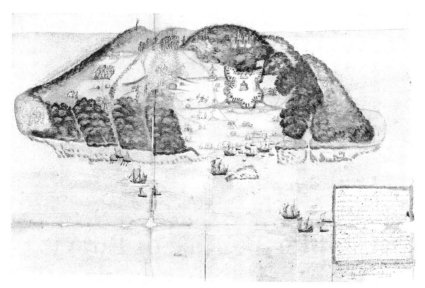

Drawing of Tortuga, author unknown, 17th century

https://commons.wikimedia.org/wiki/File:Tortuga17thcentury.jpg

Chapter 3 – Rise of Piracy: Prominent Pirates and Their Exploits

With the Golden Age encompassing three-fourths of a century, it had no shortage of well-known pirates, and their exploits would become legendary even in their own time. However, historians run into a few problems when it comes to exploring the subject of piracy. First and foremost, the contemporary records on these brigands are scarce; they are often quite barren and lacking in substance, and more often than not, they would be one-sided or even full of fiction. We will focus on the mythical image of the pirate in the later chapters, but for now, let's focus on the problem of "pinning down" the prominent sea bandits of the era. As stated, most of what we know from these pirates comes from criminal records of the era, as well as local news sources, naval reports, and the scant diaries and journals found aboard some of these vessels. In addition, locating the remains of these men is often an exercise in futility considering how many of them died at sea. Furthermore, it's difficult to locate some of their original ships due to the same problem; if a ship was decommissioned at the time, it would either be broken down for scrap parts or sunk to the bottom of the ocean. A rather large number of such pirate ships was actually located and extracted from the ocean for research, but such efforts are rare, expensive, and still don't provide a complete picture of what pirates might have been like.

In order to best cover the entire Golden Age, it's best to break it down period by period, covering some of the most prominent names that sailed the high seas and robbed wealthy ships of their precious cargo. The list will overwhelmingly deal with English pirates since they were the most prominent brigands at sea during this period. However, it will also go over several key individuals from contemporary France and the Netherlands, mostly ones active during the earliest part of the Golden Age.

The Buccaneering Period (1650–1680)

The 1650s were a time of turmoil and unease for Europe. While the major maritime powers were at peace, there was still a lot of friction between Catholic Spain and the increasingly Protestant countries like England, France, and the Netherlands. Eager to deal with the local non-Hispanic populace, the Spanish began to invade many islands in the Caribbean in an attempt to force the foreigners out. Hispaniola's French population of hunters, who were at the time called buccaneers, had to flee and establish a base on the small island of Tortuga. By the time the 1650s rolled in, these former hunters and meat smokers were already actively attacking Spanish galleons and making life a living hell for them, with the first supposed attacker to do this being a French sailor called Pierre le Grand. The adjective "supposed" needs to be stressed, as only a single source mentions this pirate by name, and he is not found anywhere else in historical records of the time. Consequently, the man who would reference this buccaneer was a buccaneer and a seafarer himself, one Alexandre Exquemelin. Though he is extremely important for this particular period of the Golden Age of Piracy, we will be covering him in a later chapter.

Up until the 1680s rolled in, the buccaneers were not only raising hell in the Caribbean, but they also found themselves invading and plundering the coastal and continental cities in Central and South America. In fact, they would often invade the same cities multiple times, often with brutal and bloody results. The number of buccaneers only increased with the English capture of Jamaica in 1655. Interestingly enough, the original mission that Oliver

Cromwell gave the two English commanders, Admiral William Penn and General Robert Venables, was to lead a surprise attack on the Spanish territories in the Caribbean, which the two men failed at spectacularly. Them capturing Jamaica was, in reality, more of an afterthought, and when the two men returned to England to report on their failures, Cromwell had them both imprisoned. However, the capture of Jamaica proved to be a step in the right direction; fifteen years later, Spain would officially cede the island to the English Crown, thus allowing both legal and illegal enterprises on the island to flourish.

As early as the 1660s, both the English governors of Jamaica at Port Royal and the French governors at Tortuga would provide letters of marque to both ex- and current buccaneers. With this documentation, the seafarers had legal backing when it came to raiding Spanish ships, though this didn't necessarily prevent them from raiding crafts of their country or its allies. The buccaneers of the time had set certain trends that would become common practice with the pirates who followed, and in terms of sheer gruesomeness or boldness, it's incredibly difficult to differentiate which generation of pirates was worse. So, it would be instructive to take a look at some of these pirates and what made them stand out.

Sir Christopher Myngs

A vice admiral with a successful career, Sir Christopher Myngs was a complex individual with an incredible life. As early as the 1650s, he was already in the Caribbean, attacking Spanish vessels and raking in a decent amount of booty. Even in these early days, Myngs was earning his infamy as a cruel, brutal commander who encouraged his men to rape and pillage as often as possible during each raid. But more importantly, Myngs had developed a questionable yet undeniably effective practice of hiring buccaneers and commanding large fleets of ships. With these men of ill-repute as his allies, Myngs successfully sacked several important cities on the South American continent, including regions of New Granada (modern-day Colombia), such as Tolú and Santa Maria, and the cities of Cumaná, Puerto Cabello, and Coro. He conducted this last series of raids in 1659.

The Spanish urged Cromwell's government to do something about Myngs, and while the English paid no heed to the Spanish pleas, Myngs would see some form of justice the same year he managed to sack three key Spanish settlements. Namely, the Jamaican governor at the time, Edward D'Oyley, urged the captain not to share his loot from the raids with the buccaneers, which Myngs ignored. Over a quarter of a million pounds went to the pirates who helped Myngs with his efforts, a hefty sum that the officials deemed worthy of an embezzlement charge. Myngs was arrested and sent to England for trial, but with Cromwell dead and the Restoration taking place, he was pardoned and offered a position as a naval officer again. Late 1662 saw him back in the Caribbean, and while the English and the Spanish were no longer at war, he was still allowed to plunder Spanish ships, which he intended to do on a grander scale than before.

Thanks to the efforts and encouragement of the new governor of Jamaica, Thomas Hickman-Windsor, 1st Earl of Plymouth (better known as Lord Windsor), Myngs was employing buccaneers left and right, promising them infinite Spanish plunder. With his new seafaring soldiers, he sacked Santiago de Cuba, the biggest city of Cuba, and took control of it. And while this was a feat worthy of praise, especially considering how strong the Spanish defenses were, it would be his next feat the following year (1663) that would cement his name as a legend among buccaneers. During that year, Myngs assembled a massive fleet of 14 ships, which collectively held over 1,400 buccaneers of various national origins. At the time, this was easily the biggest pirate fleet ever assembled, and Myngs did it with an express purpose. In February of 1663, his fleet attacked and sacked Campeche, leaving behind a massive trail of devastation and ruin. Myngs himself was badly wounded during the attack, so he left the command to the Dutch corsair Edward Mansvelt as he retreated for a much-needed recovery. By 1664, Myngs was already back in England, his wounds healing.

The last two years of Myngs's life actually saw him receive the position of vice admiral and a subsequent knighthood for his services in the Second Anglo-Dutch War. Sadly, he would not see the end of this war, as he died in action during the Four Days' Battle, which took place between June 1st and June 4th, 1666.

Myngs's story is admittedly astounding, though it pales in comparisons to the vast majority of the other pirates represented in the passages that follow. However, his life is vital for the story of the Golden Age of Piracy for two important reasons. First and foremost, the fact that he was knighted and received a high naval position shows that pirates could sometimes manage to leave their past behind and continue their lives as, more or less, law-abiding citizens. In that regard, however, Myngs is a rarity, considering that the average pirate's fate was death. The other major reason behind Myngs's importance is his willingness to employ and encourage buccaneers. During his more famous raids, sacks, plunders, and attacks, some of the most famous pirate captains and buccaneers came to prominence, and he was arguably the biggest influence on the early Golden Age pirates to increase their area of operations.

Henry Morgan

To anyone who has tasted the famous Captain Morgan rum, the naming of this beverage should be no surprise, nor should the rather flamboyant and larger-than-life image of a pirate adorning the drink. This rum was, after all, named in honor of one of the most famous buccaneers of the early Golden Age of Piracy. Arguably, the man known as Henry Morgan might be the first-ever archetypal pirate "superstar" and the first person in the illegal trade to achieve both instant infamy and widespread popularity, even during his own time.

Henry Morgan was a Welsh sailor born sometime in 1635. It's still not known how he made it to the Caribbean, but early accounts suggest that he served under Sir Christopher Myngs shortly before the sack of Campeche. He would also serve under Edward Mansfield, a seasoned privateer who had the backing of Sir Thomas Modyford, the governor of Jamaica in 1664 and the man who would provide Morgan with the letter of marque and instructions to attack Spanish settlements. (Ironically, Modyford was appointed governor with the task of reining in piratical, privateering, and buccaneering activity, and initially, he was incredibly strict and brutal in this practice but more or less completely flipped on the issue soon after.) Of course, Modyford would not be the first governor to support Morgan in his endeavors. In fact, Modyford's predecessor was none other than Edward Morgan, Henry's uncle and the father of Henry's cousin and future wife, Mary. These connections gave Henry Morgan unlimited access to local resources and support in his future privateering endeavors. Interestingly enough, Edward Morgan would go on to conquer the Dutch-held islands of Sint Eustatius and Saba in 1665; he would die in December of that same year. The control of these two islands went to yet another Morgan; this time, it was Henry's cousin and Edward's other nephew, Thomas.

Henry Morgan made use of these connections well. His first major successes were the invasions of Puerto Principe and Porto Bello, modern-day Cuba and Panama, respectively. His letter of marque, however, did not allow him to attack people on land, only at sea. He circumvented this rule by letting Modyford know that the Spanish were planning a future invasion of English lands in the Caribbean and that his own attacks were preemptive in nature. The 1668 invasion of Porto Bello, in particular, was a stunning affair. Morgan achieved this feat by having his men paddle several miles on twenty-three small canoes and invade the city at dawn. While there were some casualties, Porto Bello was taken rather quickly, and Morgan immediately held it for ransom, demanding 350,000 pesos from the president of Panama, Don Agustin. The president tried to recapture the city, but having failed in his endeavor, he resorted to bargaining with Morgan and renegotiating the ransom down to 100,000 pesos. Of course, Morgan had plundered the city dry by that point, taking anywhere between £75,000 and £100,000 of both money and goods to Modyford in Port Royal. Having overstepped the boundaries of his letter of marque, Morgan was reprimanded by Modyford, with the governor even writing to King Charles II letting him know of Morgan's disreputable ways. However, the English public, both in Jamaica and back home in London, hailed Morgan as a hero.

Morgan would go on to attack two settlements on Lake Maracaibo in modern-day Venezuela, those being the towns of Maracaibo and La Ceiba (modern-day Gibraltar, not to be confused with Gibraltar in Europe). The events at both Maracaibo and Gibraltar saw Morgan and his men enter and ransack an empty city, invade another city, retreat due to the Spanish counterattack back at Maracaibo, negotiate a retreat with no result, and then attack and utterly beat the Spanish. And to add insult to injury, he escaped back to Port Royal with the loot from both cities and the ravaged

Spanish fleet. Unfortunately, King Charles II's government would move on with a pro-Spanish stance in the late 1660s, which prompted Modyford to admonish Morgan for his acts but not arrest him outright.

What followed was probably Henry Morgan's most infamous sacking of a city: the partially successful sack of Panama, which took place between 1669 and 1672. Once again, Morgan proved himself a master tactician, using guerilla methods and the element of surprise to invade the city. In order to leave no corner unturned, Morgan assembled as many as thirty ships and one thousand men— a massive fleet that outdid even his former employer, Sir Christopher Myngs. The result was a massive rout, with only about fifteen privateers dying compared to at least four hundred Spanish men. However, Morgan would not enjoy the spoils of war as he intended. Following the orders of Panama's governor, most of the city's wealth was burned in a massive fire caused by an explosion from hidden caches of gunpowder. A huge portion of wealth was also hauled away by ships out of the city. Morgan took off with what was left, which was still not a small sum at the time, but it was far lower than what the privateers had been expecting from a city as big as Panama.

As was the case with his previous raids, Morgan was accused of torture and other crimes, as well as retaining most of the loot and not providing the allotted share to the Crown. He was arrested alongside Modyford and sent to England in 1672, but as soon as he touched English soil, he was hailed as a hero and even knighted. Morgan would go back to Jamaica in 1675 and live out his days as a plantation owner until his death on August 25th, 1688. He would be actively involved in Jamaican politics, even serving as the governor of the island on three separate occasions.

Interestingly, Henry Morgan, though being the epitome of a pirate in the early Golden Age, vehemently refused to be addressed as such. He was a privateer, and according to his own words, he vehemently hated pirates, buccaneers, and the like. He even publicly refuted most of the accusations that were levied against him, especially ones that referred to his supposed torture of locals, misuse of nuns and other religious figures during his raid of Porto Bello, and embezzling money after each raid. In fact, Alexandre

Exquemelin, who wrote about the Welsh privateer, lost a very public lawsuit, and publishers were forced to retract some of the information from future printings of Exquemelin's works. But no matter what Henry Morgan called himself, he was far from a clean privateer who stuck to his letter of marque.

Henry Morgan sacking Puerto Principe in 1668

David Marteen

David Marteen was a Dutch privateer, and he was known as one of the people who willingly joined Henry Morgan in his raid of Spanish settlements in Central and South America, collectively known as the Spanish Main. Taking a contingent of men in 1664,

Marteen sacked Villa Hermosa (modern Villahermosa) in the Tabasco province in a surprise raid after having marched fifty miles inland to do so. Upon his return, he had to face the Spanish patrol and retake the ships they had captured. His raids continued in Central America after this incident, with the sack of the city of Granada, Nicaragua, being the last one before Marteen departed in 1665. In the coming years, he would serve Governor Modyford as a privateer, a career he continued even under Modyford's successor, Governor Thomas Lynch.

Marteen is not particularly famous for his raids, brutality, or eccentricity, unlike many of the other pirates covered in this volume. However, he is significant to overall pirate lore and history as being one of the first men at sea who was rumored to have buried his valuables, thus creating the legend of the so-called "buried pirate treasure." Supposedly, Marteen set up camp near Salmon Brook in modern-day Connecticut, United States, sometime in 1655, a little after raiding the Spanish galleon *Neptune*. However, the locals did not appreciate the pirate's presence there, so he and his crew sailed away, burying vast amounts of their wealth at the spot. Other sources even claim that Marteen's men established a full-fledged settlement that was wiped out more than two decades later. However, nothing in the historical records suggests an event like this happened, and Marteen probably never even sailed anywhere close to Connecticut.

Laurens de Graaf

Laurens de Graaf was a Dutch privateer who spent most of his life in the service of the French Caribbean colony of Saint-Domingue (modern-day Haiti). His early life is somewhat obscure, with the most likely account being that he was sold into slavery and worked on a plantation in the Canary Islands. He somehow escaped his capture, married his French-born wife in 1674, then moved to the Caribbean and started as a privateer in the service of the French soon after. In fact, there are even some records of him helping a raid of Campeche in 1672, two years before his marriage and well before he made the Caribbean his permanent place of residence. During the late 1670s, he managed to capture a large number of ships, each larger than the last, and converted all of their crews to piracy. His biggest early success was capturing a Spanish frigate from the imposing Armada de Barlovento (a huge Spanish force of fifty ships that had the task of overseeing Spanish American territories and protecting them from advances of other nations) in 1679. By the early 1680s, he had become so prominent that Henry Morgan himself, during one of his stints as a governor, sent a pirate-hunting frigate after him.

De Graaf's career in piracy, however, had only just begun. The Spanish decided to take vengeance for their armada's defeat and the loss of a ship, but de Graaf took them head-on and defeated them after a prolonged sea battle. Soon enough, he would ally himself, albeit reluctantly, with another Dutch privateer, Nicholas van Hoorn. The two men forged a plan to sack the city of Veracruz (in modern-day Mexico). Their plan came to fruition on May 17th, 1683. However, the two men would end up in a massive quarrel not long after. With the Spanish fleet appearing to help the people of Veracruz, de Graaf and van Hoorn retreated to a nearby island called Isla de Sacrificios with the hostages. There, they shared the spoils and waited for the ransom on the hostages to be paid out. However, van Hoorn grew impatient and executed multiple hostages, sending their heads to the Spanish as a consequence of not receiving the ransom on time. This act infuriated de Graaf, who was by no means an angel (in fact, the Spanish would see de Graaf as the Devil incarnate), but he was firmly against the mistreatment of hostages. The two supposedly fought a duel over the matter, and while no man died, van Hoorn was wounded. His wound would soon fester and grow gangrenous, and he died not long after.

This willingness to treat the hostages well was not new behavior for de Graaf, and he would exhibit it again when his men wanted to tear into their prisoners during the Dutch privateer's second sack of Campeche in 1685. He would go on to fight the Spanish for a few more years, leading attacks in Cuba, but at some point, he also started going after English ships. He remarried, in the meantime, to a female buccaneer called Anne Dieu-le-Veut. Around 1695, the English launched counter-offensives on de Graaf, beating his fleet and capturing his family after an attack on Port-de-Paix in Saint-Domingue. De Graaf's later whereabouts are a mystery to historians, with one plausible outcome being that he died in Louisiana while helping to establish a French colony there.

De Graaf's life, much like Marteen's, doesn't seem too important on the face of it when we compare it to other pirates who came after him. However, his naval battle against the Spanish would inspire the long-standing trope of massive pirate naval battles with swords, musket fire, and huge cannonades. Like most things regarding the subject of pirates, the idea of naval battles was blown out of proportion, and de Graaf's skirmish with the armada was the exception, not the rule. But de Graaf also inspired another pirate myth, that of honorable pirate duels. While dueling was generally seen as a way to settle the score, it was nowhere near as dramatic or impressive as the one between de Graaf and van Hoorn. In fact, it was rare for two pirate captains to go at it; the majority of said pirate duels happened between regular sailors, mostly over sharing the spoils of a raid.

Nicholas van Hoorn

As we saw earlier, Nicholas van Hoorn would inevitably die due to the consequences of his duel with Laurens de Graaf. And indeed, the previous attack on Veracruz was the highlight of his career. However, it was merely the crowning moment of what were decades of successful seafaring notoriety, both as a privateer and as an outright pirate.

Van Hoorn was, at first, enlisted in the service of France, attacking both Dutch and Spanish ships, but he would soon turn on his own masters and go after French ships as well. In fact, van Hoorn was so infamous yet so effective that all three countries would employ his services at one point or another. During the early 1680s, he was known for plundering the west coast of African in search of slaves. His escapades became well known in the Caribbean, and the English were on his tail, though nothing came of their pursuits. Van Hoorn would soon reach the French part of Hispaniola and gain a letter of marque from its governor, enabling him to go after the Spanish settlements—an endeavor that ultimately led to the sacking of Veracruz and his famous episode with Laurens de Graaf.

In terms of infamy, van Hoorn was far from benevolent. Considering that he was capable of turning against his employers if a better opportunity arose, he was one of those contemporary pirates who perfectly fit the stereotypical depiction of a buccaneer. He was, however, far from being one of the worst to emerge during this era.

François L'Olonnais

Millions of people worldwide are aware of a particular Japanese manga called *One Piece*. Since its inception, this story of Monkey D. Luffy and his fellow pirates has sold close to five hundred million volumes, and it's still an ongoing series and a huge media empire. Sharp-eyed fans will, of course, know about one particular member of the *One Piece* cast, a particularly rugged, manly, dangerous sword-wielder named Roronoa Zoro. What most fans probably don't know is that he was the only member of Luffy's crew who was named after a real-life pirate, a buccaneer who is arguably far more gruesome and deadly than his manga counterpart.

François L'Olonnais, whose real name is Jean-David Nau, was most likely born in the small French town of Les Sables-d'Olonne (hence his nom de guerre, "the Frenchman of Olonne") and was sold as an indentured servant in the Caribbean early in his life. After his servitude expired in 1660, he began sailing around the Caribbean islands until finally settling in Saint-Domingue, where he became a buccaneer. The most fateful event of this period was when L'Olonnais shipwrecked near Campeche around 1661 or 1662, which was followed by the Spanish massacring his entire crew. He survived by supposedly covering himself in blood and hiding among the dead. Once he managed to depart Campeche, he settled in Tortuga. Not long after, he held a Spanish town hostage with a group of other buccaneers. Once the Spanish sent out a ship to deal with him, he ordered every single crew member to be beheaded save for one. That one man was to relay a message to the Spanish authorities, which more than explained L'Olonnais's *raison d'être* from that point forward—"I shall never henceforward give quarter to any Spaniard whatsoever."

True to his word, L'Olonnais would go on many raiding parties against the Spanish in the Caribbean and the surrounding continental lands. His most famed raid was the ransacking of Maracaibo, modern-day Venezuela, in 1666. The rape of this city took place over a few months, with L'Olonnais and his men torturing, raping, and killing its inhabitants with cruel and brutal proficiency. His next target was Gibraltar, and despite the city's protection by a Spanish force that greatly outnumbered the buccaneers, L'Olonnais managed to beat them and hold the city for ransom. Despite getting said ransom, the French pirate still looted the city, and the inhabitants were left in a state of utter chaos. News of L'Olonnais's brutality quickly spread throughout the Caribbean, and he was aptly dubbed the "Bane of Spain."

However, his most brutal reported act (if it really happened since there's only one source mentioning it) came to pass when L'Olonnais and his men were pillaging through what is now modern-day Honduras. After raiding the city of Puerto Cavallo and moving onto San Pedro, the buccaneers were ambushed by the Spanish and only barely managed to escape. L'Olonnais took two Spanish prisoners with him, and while he was interrogating them for a safe, clear route to San Pedro, he cut open one of them, tore his heart out, and gnawed at it right in front of everyone's eyes.

His subsequent exploits saw him attacking other Spanish-held cities, such as Campeche, Guatemala, and San Pedro Sula, and he even managed to sail to Jamaica and sell one of his old ships to a fellow buccaneer. Interestingly, L'Olonnais's death came not at the hands of the Spanish but of native tribes that lived in Central America. Somewhere in modern-day Panama, L'Olonnais and his men were captured by the Darién in 1669, and those natives were, in turn, captured by the Kuna. The Kuna actually killed L'Olonnais and, according to scarce sources, dismembered his body and burned the remains.

Few men were as feared as François L'Olonnais, and if there's one thing that his life proves without a shadow of a doubt, it's that an effective pirate captain who wanted to maintain his position needed to have either immense charisma, perfect leadership skills, or the ability to terrify everyone on board beyond belief. This point will become relevant later when we cover the everyday life of pirates during the Golden Age.

Roche Braziliano

As stated earlier, François L'Olonnais managed to sail all the way to Jamaica and sell one of his old ships to a fellow buccaneer. It just so happened that this buccaneer, a Dutchman whose real name is still a matter of historical debate, shared a lot of the same traits as his French counterpart, and though his career is not as well-known as that of L'Olonnais, he has nonetheless remained one of the most brutal Dutch pirates of the early Golden Age.

The man known as Roche Braziliano (with many alternative spellings; consequently, the lack of a single proper spelling for pirate names was common during the Golden Age, nor was taking up pseudonyms) was an exile living in Brazil, parts of which were controlled by the Dutch at the time. Braziliano started his privateering career there, soon moving to the Caribbean and capturing scores of ships. During his activities in the West Indies, he was captured, arrested, and sent to Spain. Upon his escape, he swore that he would end his enemies, sharing the same burning hatred for the Spanish as the man from whom he would later buy a ship.

With his new ship, Braziliano was ready to do some raiding, and throughout the 1660s, he would sail under the command of none other than Henry Morgan during one of his many raids into the Spanish Main. Much like L'Olonnais, Braziliano enjoyed torturing his captives, with one brutal example being him roasting Spaniards alive over an open fire. Braziliano was also known to be a loud, obnoxious drunk who was willing to kill a man who wouldn't drink with him. His booming buccaneering career, however, ended somewhat abruptly after 1671, as all traces of his activities disappear.

Braziliano shared his cruelty with L'Olonnais, and that's what initially made him infamous. However, his real claim to legacy is his drunkenness. It is a well-known stereotype that pirates love to get drunk both on and off duty, and indeed, it was one stereotype that held true in the vast majority of cases, with some notable exceptions. Of all the recorded pirates in the early Golden Age, Braziliano was certainly the biggest drunkard and quite possibly even the proudest of that fact.

The Pirate Round Period (the 1690s)

As the 17th century was nearing its end, the major maritime forces increased their efforts in reducing piracy in the Caribbean. Furthermore, with the Glorious Revolution of 1688 taking place and William of Orange taking the throne of England, the country renewed its hostilities with France and its eccentric king, Louis XIV. And while that topic is fascinating in and of itself, it's merely the backdrop behind the first collapse of the buccaneering period of the

Golden Age. Namely, the Brethren of the Coast was an international crew of people, and once hostilities between England and France reignited, the men simply refused to collaborate with one another. In other words, gone were the days when Henry Morgan could lead a raid with dozens of ships sailing under many different colors. Furthermore, the cities in the Spanish Main and on the islands were drained of their resources. Piracy did continue, but the sea brigands needed a new, fresh pool of resources. And they did, indeed, find one, hundreds of miles away, near the eastern shores of Africa.

There was no better time to sail the Indian Ocean than the 1690s. The Indian subcontinent and the surrounding lands were laden with resources that Europeans craved at the time, such as silk, calico, tea, spices, and even art. Furthermore, South and Southeast Asia housed several dozens of factories from a few East India companies from Europe, and the ships coming and going to these factories would often carry valuables on board and even years' worth of wages for each factory worker. And considering how thinly the European maritime forces were spread at the time, policing these waters was a task doomed to fail, as everyone, from a small fishing boat to a huge trading galleon, was a target for pirates. And it didn't just stop with European ships. Vessels sent out by the Great Moghul would also find themselves on the pirates' radar, and considering the vast wealth of the Moghuls, plundering their vessels would be quite lucrative. That's why European pirates also found themselves in the Red Sea, which was a popular trading spot for both the Mughal Empire and the local Muslim merchants (either Arabian or Ottoman).

The lengthy route that the pirates would take from either the Caribbean or Europe to the Indian subcontinent had a fitting name: the Pirate Round. And while the period of the Pirate Round was the briefest of all three that encompass the Golden Age, it was probably more significant than the buccaneering period. After all, it was the pirates who made up this period that showed the world just how alluring, engaging, and profitable the pirate trade could be. But more importantly, it helped put piracy on the map as an issue the major powers could no longer ignore.

Thomas Tew

Thomas Tew, an English seafarer born somewhere in the American colonies, might not have had a career that involved countless voyages and city sackings like his buccaneering predecessors did. In fact, he only made two significant pirate cruises in his entire life. However, not only was he successful in being a pirate, but he was also arguably the progenitor of the Pirate Round, as he was the first pirate to show the immense possibilities of sailing east rather than west.

Tew began his career in the early 1690s in Bermuda, where he had obtained a letter of marque to go after French settlements in the current-day Republic of The Gambia in West Africa. However, shortly after sailing on this journey, Tew openly declared to his crew that he wanted to turn to piracy. According to reports, his crew accepted this change of pace with open arms, and his ship, the *Amity*, set sail for the Red Sea.

Once there, Tew and his men attacked a rather large dhow (a type of single or multiple mast ship common in that region; the particular dhow that Tew went after was a ghanjah), and he did so with no casualties on either side; the dhow crew simply surrendered. Tew's plunder was massive, with his own share of the loot being valued at anywhere between £5,000 and £8,000 in contemporary currency. He and his men divided the plunder when they docked at Madagascar to careen the ship (flip it on the side during the low tide for necessary repairs) before sailing onward to New York. Interestingly, they docked in Île Sainte-Marie, where Adam Baldridge (another pirate who will be covered later on) had built a sturdy fort and hosted numerous pirates over the years.

Back after his first successful pirate run, Tew became close friends with Benjamin Fletcher, the governor of New York. He would finance another of Tew's expeditions in 1694. Tew was back at the mouth of the Red Sea, but this time, he found it swarming with other notable pirates. His story, it seems, had become widespread, so everyone wanted a piece of the new Pirate Round. Tew, among many other captains, decided to sail under another famed seafarer at the time, Henry Every. Tew's ship actually attacked a vessel from a powerful Mughal convoy, with Tew believing that they were going after the famous *Fateh Muhammed*, a particularly wealthy ship with bountiful plunder. However, during the skirmish, Tew lost his life. However, the story doesn't end there. His men, demoralized after his death, surrendered to the Mughal forces, though they would later be rescued by none other than Henry Every during his own successes over the Muslim ships. One of Tew's crew members, a pirate known as John Ireland, took the *Amity* to Baldridge's pirate safe haven to have the ship refitted. Both Thomas Tew and John Ireland had been targets of Captain William Kidd, at least according to the commission he had received from King William III.

Thomas Tew was undoubtedly important for pioneering the Pirate Round cruises and plunders, and though he did not enjoy the fruits of his crew's final plunder, he was nonetheless effective throughout his life. Furthermore, Tew became the source of another famous pirate myth, that of a seafarer getting involved with a native woman of royalty and producing offspring. According to legend, Tew had an affair with a Malagasy princess, and as a result, his son, Ratsimilaho, was born. The boy would use this supposed familial connection to rule over a large region in the island known as the Betsimisaraka confederation. Of course, it's unknown if Ratsimilaho was actually the son of a pirate and a queen, and even if he was, only the first name of the pirate is given, that being "Thomas." Considering how common of a name that was in contemporary England, his piratical father could have been anyone, Tew included. Of course, pirates and native Malagasy women often intermarried and interbred, so it wasn't all that rare for their offspring to play prominent roles in Malagasy sociopolitical events.

Henry Every

Western history gained its first "Arch Pirate" in 1694. This man would only be an active pirate for roughly two years, but he still achieved the seemingly impossible: he acquired a massive amount of wealth from a huge raid of important Mughal ships and managed to escape justice unscathed. If Thomas Tew inspired people to turn pirate and rob the ships in the Indian Ocean and the Red Sea, the honor of catapulting piracy into the stuff of legends belonged to none other than a clean-shaven, stocky, pale-faced man of a medium, unimposing height with piercing cold eyes: Henry Every.

Every's birthplace was most likely a village in England known as Newton Ferrers, some distance away from Plymouth. Based on his skills, it's likely that he had seafaring experiences at a fairly young age. Some legends claim that he fought in the waters around Algiers and Campeche and around the Caribbean in the 1670s, but none of that can be substantiated by historical evidence. The earliest record we have of Every's activities was during the Nine Years' War between France and England. Every was a midshipman on the HMS *Rupert* in his early thirties; by this time, he was already married with a family to support. In 1690, he participated in various battles, including the infamous Battle of Beachy Head. Soon after, he was discharged from the navy. Following his discharge, Every began his early illegal enterprises, sailing as an interloper (i.e., an unlicensed slaver). He had the sneaky habit of capturing both the slaves and their former slaveowners.

In 1694, Every's inevitable turn to piracy took place when he was elected as the first mate of *Charles II*, one of four ships that were part of the so-called Spanish Expedition Shipping venture. The venture's goal was to expand trade with the Spanish and prey on the French ships in the Caribbean. However, due to a series of misfortunes and due to *Charles II*'s Captain Gibson being an unreliable drunk, the men soon started to talk about mutiny. Every spearheaded the movement, and the men indeed mutinied and marooned Gibson onshore, taking *Charles II* and renaming it the *Fancy*. Unsurprisingly, Every was elected captain of the ship.

Every began his piratical career in Cape Verde, attacking three English merchant ships and recruiting some men to his crew. After a few brief stints on the Guinea coast and at Benin, where he had his ship fitted to sail faster, Every moved to the island of Principe, where he captured two Danish privateers and added more men to his crew. Near the Comoro Islands, specifically the island of Johanna, Every captured a French pirate ship, looted it, and recruited more men, with his force now rounding up to a neat 150 men. But this was all merely preparation for his biggest success to date, if not the single biggest success in the history of the Golden Age of Piracy.

Entering the Mandab Strait (modern-day Bab-el-Mandeb) into the Red Sea, Every ran into five other pirate captains: Richard

Want, William Mayes, Joseph Faro, Thomas Wake, and the aforementioned Thomas Tew. The men agreed to unite their ships into a massive fleet, with Every as the admiral, in order to capture a convoy of twenty-five Mughal ships. The two biggest ships of the empire were part of the convoy, with the 600-ton *Fateh Muhammed* (the one Tew lost his life and crew to) being the escort to a far larger, far fiercer ship that was the pride and joy of the Great Moghul: the 1,600-ton, 80-cannon strong *Ganj-i-Sawai* ("exceeding treasure"). After about five days of pursuit and the loss of the *Amity's* crew and captain, Every managed to capture *Fateh Muhammed*, whose own crew gave up without any resistance. *Ganj-i-Sawai*, however, put up a massive resistance, which resulted in a fierce battle.

Every was incredibly lucky in at least two instances during the battle. The first instance was during his initial attack when the *Fancy* struck the broadside of *Ganj-i-Sawai's* mainmast, damaging it significantly. His next stroke of luck came from some of the cannons on board the Mughal ship exploding, which killed or seriously injured a huge number of crew members on board. Every reportedly ordered his men to loot, rape, and pillage as ruthlessly as possible, with some of the Muslim women on board who were part of the royal entourage reportedly killing themselves by jumping overboard into the sea to avoid becoming rape victims. An unsubstantiated legend suggests that Mughal Emperor Aurangzeb's own granddaughter was on board and that Every had his way with her. While most of these tales of brutality are exaggerated, there was a lot of illicit behavior aboard the captured *Ganj-i-Sawai*, at least according to the testimonies of Every's crew members, who were arrested years later.

The spoils from both *Ganj-i-Sawai* and *Fateh Muhammed* made Every and his men rich beyond their wildest dreams. However, what ensued was a veritable death sentence to every single one of the pirates involved with this raid. Once the stripped *Ganj-i-Sawai* made its way to the Indian shores, the local governors immediately briefed Emperor Aurangzeb of the situation, and they imprisoned the English East India Company (EIC) factors in the meantime. Beside himself with absolute rage, Aurangzeb forced the closures of four separate EIC factories and put their officers behind bars. He almost went as far as to attack the English-controlled city of Bombay.

Both British Parliament and the EIC had to find a way to appease the Great Moghul since their East Indian trade quite literally depended on his good spirits. As such, an award of £500, later to be doubled at £1,000, was offered for the capture of Henry Every, thus beginning the first-ever worldwide manhunt in history. And fate would have it that this manhunt ended in failure; after 1696, there are no reliable records of Henry Every's activities anywhere. There were some rumors that he either spent the rest of his days in Madagascar, lived in England alongside the Great Moghul's granddaughter, or wasted away in the English countryside, dying destitute. Whatever the case may be, one thing is for sure—Every remains one of the few pirates to have completely escaped facing justice and paying for his crimes, thus cementing him as the "Arch Pirate."

The historical importance of Henry Every cannot be overstated. And like many other pirates, he also pioneered, or rather improved upon, the trend of using false names and aliases. To many crews on the open sea, he was known either as John or Jack Avery, Benjamin Bridgeman, or Long Ben. This last alias, in particular, was a favorite of his crew and associates.

PROCLAMATION

For Apprehending Henry Every, alias Bridgeman, and sundry other Pirates.

ILLIAM By the Grace of GOD, King of Great-Britain, France and Ireland, Defender of the Faith, To

Macers of Our Privy Council, Messengers at Arms, Our Sheriffs in that part Conjunctly and severally, specially Constitute Greeting. For as much as, We are Informed that Henry Every, alias Bridgeman, together with several other Persons, English Men, Scots Men, and Foraigners, to the Number of about One Hundred and Thirty, did Steal, and Run away with the Ship called the Phanse, alias Charles, of Fourty six Guns from the Port of Corunna in Spain, and Commit several Acts of Pyrracy under English Colours upon the Seas of India or Persia Contrary to the Law of Nations, and of this Kingdom in particular; And that the said Henry Every, and severals of his Accomplices, since Committing of the saids Acts of Pyrracy, having left the said Ship in the Island of Providence, are Returned to, and have Dispersed themselves within this Our antient Kingdom, thinking, and Intending thereby to Save & Shelter themselves from the Punishment & Execution of Law Due to such Hainous and Notorious Offenders: And We being Resolved, that outmost Diligence shall be Used for Seizing, and Apprehending the Persons of such Open and Villanous Transgressors; Do therefore, with Advice of the Lords of Our Privy Council, Require, and Command, the Sheriffs of the several Shires, Stewarts of Stewartries, Baillies of Regalities, and their Respective Deputs, Magistrats of Burghs, Officers of Our Army, Commanders of Our Forces and Garisons, and all others Imployed, or Trusted by Us in any Station whatsoever, Civil or Military within this Kingdom, and Our Good Subjects whatsoever within the same, to do their outmost Indeavour and Diligence to Seize upon, and Apprehend the Persons of the said Henry Every, alias Bridgeman, together with James Cray, Thomas Summerton, Edward Kirwood, William Down, John Reddy, John Stroger, Nathaniel Pike, Peter Soans, Henry Adams, Francis Frennier, Thomas Johnson, Joseph Dawson, Samuel Dawson, James Lewis, John Sparks, Joseph Goss, Charles Falconer, James Murray, Robert Rich, John Miler, John King, Edward Savil, William Philips, Thomas Jope, and Thomas Belisse his Accomplices, or any of them, and such others as were with them in the said Ship (who may be Probably known and Discovered by the Great Quantities of Persian and Indian Gold and Silver which they have with them) and Deliver him or them Prisoners to the next Magistrat of any of Our Burghs, to be by them keeped in safe Custody until farther Order be taken for bringing him or them to such Condign Punishment as their Crime does Deserve, and out of Detestation to such a Horrid villany, and to the Effect the same may not go Un-punished; and for Incouraging the Magistrats above-named, and any other of Our Good Subjects to Search for, and Apprehend such Nottorious Rogues: We with Advice foresaid do make Offer, and Assure the Payment of the Sum of Five Hundred Pounds Sterling for the said Henry Every, alias Bridgeman, and Fiftieth Pounds Sterling Money foresaid for every one of the other Persons above-named to any Person or Persons who shall Seize and Apprehend them or any of them, and Deliver him or them Prisoners to any of the Magistrats of Our Burghs, which shall be Truely and Faithfully payed, as a Reward to the said Person or Persons who shall Apprehend and Deliver Prisoner to any of Our Magistrats the. saids Henry Every, or any other of his Accomplices above-named, Indemnifying hereby all and every one of Our Subjects from any Hazard of Slaughter, Mutilation, or other Acts of Violence which they may Commit against the said Henry Every, or any of his Accomplices, or any Persons that shall Assist them, to Hinder and Oppose their being Seized and Taken: And We with Advice foresaid Peremptorly Inhibit and Discharge all, and every one of Our Subjects whatsomever to Shelter, Harbour, Conceal, or any ways Assist, or Supply the said Henry Every, or any of his Accomplices above-named upon their Highest Peril, OUR WILL IS HEREFORE, and We Charge you Strictly, and Command, that Incontinent these Our Letters seen, ye pass to the Mercat-Corss of Edinburgh, and Remanent Mercat Crosses of the Head-Burghs of the several Shires and Stewartries within this Kingdom, and there in Our Name and Authority make Intimation hereof that none may pretend Ignorance. And Ordains these Presents to be Printed.

Given under Our Signet at Edinburgh the Eighteenth Day of August, and of Our Reign the Eighth Year. 1696.

Per Actum Dominorum Secreti Concilii;
DA. MONCRIEFE. Cls. Sti. Concilii.

GOD Save the King.

Edinburgh, Printed by the Heirs and Successors of Andrew Anderson, Printer to His most Excellent Majesty, Anno DOM, 1696

Proclamation for apprehending Henry Every, 1696, Privy Council of Scotland

https://commons.wikimedia.org/wiki/File:Proclamation_for_apprehending_Henry_Every.jpg

William Kidd

Most of the famed pirates became involved with the practice willingly, mostly out of necessity. Of course, as we will see later, a few did so out of a sense of adventure and even took pride in being sea brigands. However, it was (and still is) incredibly difficult to find someone who became a pirate by way of an odd cosmic coincidence. It's also rare to have an infamous, influential pirate who vehemently refused to be referred to as one.

Despite how his story unfolded, William Kidd was not an inexperienced man in terms of sailing. In fact, he had been at sea for decades before his short-lived and turbulent stint as a pirate hunter in the late 1690s. In fact, it would be Kidd and his future crew, which included future infamous pirates such as Robert Culliford and Samuel Burgess, who would take a ship with a successful mutiny, rename it *Blessed William*, and, as privateers, go on to defend the British territory of Nevis (a small island in the Caribbean) during the early years of the War of the Great Alliance. As early as 1690, Culliford mutinied against Kidd and stole the ship, sailing away with it to Madagascar.

By the time 1695 rolled around the corner, Kidd was living the good life in New York; he was well in his forties and married to Sarah Bradley Cox Oort, a twice-widowed woman who was one of the richest people in the city at the time. In December of the aforementioned year, Kidd received a letter of marque from Richard Coote, 1st Earl of Bellomont, who became governor of New York, Massachusetts, and New Hampshire, for a pirate-hunting mission. Kidd was to apprehend notorious pirates, including Thomas Tew, who sailed in the Pirate Round. The expedition was supported by the Whigs, a political party in England, and it was backed by a lot of powerful men of the English aristocracy. Thus, Kidd took it pretty seriously.

One of the main reasons behind Kidd's decision to accept the mission was the potential of becoming a Royal Navy commander, which he saw as his goal. His new ship, the *Adventure Galley*, was a massive vessel containing 34 cannons, and it had a crew of 150 men. Kidd personally chose his crew members based on experience, talent, and reputation. However, the first snag on his voyage supposedly came from this same crew exposing their naked rear ends to the Royal Navy yacht anchored at Greenwich, which prompted the yacht's captain to press most of Kidd's crew into naval service. Kidd had to replace his crew in New York City. He had already lost a lot of time from completing his mission, and quite a few of the new crew members were convicted felons and former criminals, so there was a high probability that a lot of them were active pirates as well.

The commission that Kidd acquired stipulated that he had to report to Lord Bellomont until March 20th, 1697. He also had permission to attack and raid French ships, considering that England was at war with France at the time. The document stipulated that 10 percent of all plunder would go directly to the Crown, with the rest being divided by his crew. King William III signed this paper himself, with some sources even implying that he financed the expedition, at least in part.

Nearly everything went wrong on Kidd's journey to the East African coast. He ran out of money and provisions quickly, but despite his crew members' protests, he vehemently refused to attack privateer ships from the Netherlands and England due to the conditions of his letter of marque. The crew was openly mutinous early on, and they would argue with Kidd frequently, with one of these fights resulting in Kidd killing his gunner, William Moore, by hitting him over the head with an ironbound bucket. The murder took place on October 30th, 1697, more than half a year past Kidd's due date.

Soon enough, Kidd would commit his first unwitting act of piracy by capturing an Indian trading vessel called *Quedagh Merchant*. The ship itself was hired by Armenian merchants, and the crew had French protection passes obtained through the French East India Company. However, the captain of the ship was an Englishman, so the capture of his ship technically still counted as a breach of Kidd's commission. The crew refused to return the stolen goods to the English captain, though, and soon enough, Kidd had to find a way to sell all of the stolen goods. He did so by sailing to a few ports in Madagascar and dealing with the local merchants, nearly all of who dealt with stolen pirate goods and who had been pirates themselves. Kidd kept both the ship and the French passes, confident that these documents would prove that he had no other choice but to attack the vessel. In the waters around Madagascar, Kidd would meet with Robert Culliford, possibly the only pirate he came across during his journey. Their meeting resulted in a huge number of Kidd's crew deserting to join Culliford.

Upon Kidd's return to the American coast, he was already a wanted man in England, and Lord Bellomont ordered his arrest on July 6th, 1699. Kidd was taken back to England soon after, and throughout his subsequent trial, he kept claiming that he was innocent of any piratical activity. The passes he had with him mysteriously vanished during the trial, and his former colleagues offered no support. It's no secret that his entire trial was used by the Tories (another political party in England) in order to discredit the Whigs who had backed Kidd and his mission. The tactic worked. Kidd was sentenced on two accounts, the first being the murder of his gunner, the second being his acts of piracy. He was hung on May 23rd, 1701, with his execution almost symbolically marking the end of the middle period of the Golden Age of Piracy.

Kidd was far from a successful or fearsome pirate, and he would vehemently refuse to call himself that, as he was convinced that everything he did was perfectly legal. But Kidd's accidental stint of piracy isn't what made him famous or a prominent figure of pirate history. In fact, it would be one particular act of his that would cement one of the biggest pirate myths. Namely, while he was returning to New York, Kidd stopped at Gardiners Island, a small territory in the Long Island Sound. After conversing with the island's proprietor, John Gardiner, Kidd reached an agreement and decided to hide some of his loot in a swamp between Bostwick Point and the island's manor. Supposedly, he buried several chests of gold and jewels. This simple act of stashing away some of his ill-gotten gains catapulted the legend of secret buried pirate treasure, a phenomenon that was so influential that people back then would head to the island and the surrounding areas in order to dig up said treasure. Of course, none of that supposed treasure was there since Bellomont ordered its confiscation during Kidd's trial.

Adam Baldridge

Adam Baldridge was one of the earliest pirates to inhabit a settlement near Madagascar and start a lucrative business trading with illicit pirate goods. He had been on the island since at least the late 1680s, having escaped there from Jamaica to evade a murder charge. He built a stockade fort that had forty guns, and it was strong enough to protect any ships from incoming enemies. Furthermore, Baldridge also traded with the natives of Madagascar. He occasionally dabbled in slavery; at one point, he even subdued the local tribes and forced the chieftains to pay tribute to him. He would dispense law locally to both the natives and the white inhabitants (most of whom were pirates), and he ruled from his home on Île Sainte-Marie, which was just as fortified and sturdy as the main fort he built. In essence, he was one of the earliest "kings of Madagascar," with his reign remaining unchecked due to his influence, affluence, and the vast number of European weapons and guns that no native could handle in an open fight. However, Baldridge would not remain in Madagascar. Some sources claim that he eventually became a legitimate businessman and that he died well in his seventies. And though he might have been one of the first de facto kings of Madagascar and its territories, he would not be the last.

The Interim Period: The War of the Spanish Succession

Between 1701 and 1714, piracy seemed to wane a bit, mainly because Europe had been engulfed in a series of massive conflicts that would determine the continent's power balance. It was actually, in a sense, a proto-world war; the main conflict took place across central, western, and southern Europe, but there were dozens of related wars in the Americas and the Indian subcontinent. In fact, the consequences of these wars would directly lead to what is known as the single most profitable, most active, and most famous period during the Golden Age of Piracy, and it all happened because of complicated European succession rights.

The Spanish king at the time, Charles II, was famously of poor health and had no heirs. During his lifetime, he named Philip of Anjou (later King Philip V), who was the grandson of French King Louis XIV, as his heir. However, Charles had familial relations with other royal houses of Europe, most notably the Austrian branch of the Habsburgs. The Habsburgs' own Archduke Charles (later Emperor Charles VI of the Holy Roman Empire) would be the next best claimant to the vacant throne of Spain, and if either of the two men, be it the French prince or the Austrian archduke, took the throne, it would have tipped the scales of power in Europe.

Multiple nations did not approve of that, especially England, which had been seeking to divide the Spanish Empire for years, mainly because the new shift in power would severely affect the English in various ways. When Philip was declared king on

November 16th, 1700, war was inevitable. The main belligerents were France and Spain, with their allies in the Italian Peninsula, Bavaria, Cologne, and Liege, on one side, and the so-called Grand Alliance (England, the Netherlands, and the Holy Roman Empire) and their allies of Portugal, Prussia, and the pro-Habsburg parts of Spain, on another. This massive battlefield spanned several continents and dragged on for almost a decade and a half, and it was appropriately named the War of the Spanish Succession. It ended with a massively divided and chaotic Europe, with all of the countries depleted of their resources and unprepared for other large conflicts, which were inevitable.

One section of the War of the Spanish Succession took place in the Americas, and it was known as the Third Indian War or Queen Anne's War in England and the Second Intercolonial War in France. During this time, the forces of France and England, each assisted by a host of native tribes across North and Central America, clashed in brutal warfare that ended with the same treaty that ended the wars in Europe, that being the Treaty of Utrecht of 1713.

An important theater of the American side of the conflict took place in the West Indies. Both the English and the French employed privateers to go after their enemy's plunder, which helped disrupt shipping and trade from the West Indies to Europe. One reason pirating waned during this period was because seafarers, who had proper and legal letters of marque, pretty much had legal carte blanche to essentially do what pirates do openly. And since a privateer could earn far more than a regular navy seaman, it was a lucrative endeavor in which a lot of men decided to partake.

However, with the wars finished and peace treaties signed, all hostilities between England and France in the colonial territories were, at least on paper, to cease. This led to a sequence of events that left contemporary men and women desperate to earn a living. Thousands of privateers were out of a job overnight, and their letters of marque were suddenly null and void. Furthermore, there were plenty of men who had participated in the wars who came out dirt-poor and devastated, with no other option but to turn to plantation work or maritime jobs. And even if they had valid letters of marque, going after Spanish ships would not amount to much considering how devastated the country had been after the war. Most importantly of all, policing along the Caribbean and the American coastlines was sparse since the majority of naval forces had been decimated during the wars; on top of that, the countries were slow to recover and rebuild. In other words, the stage was set for what was probably the best-known period of piracy in the entire recorded history of mankind.

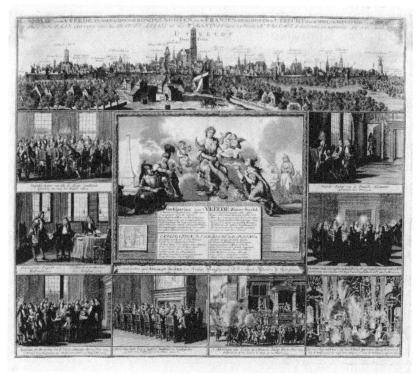

Treaty of Utrecht, 18th-century color print by Abraham Allard, Bibliothèque nationale de France

Post-Succession Period (1715–1726)

A decade might not seem that long, especially considering that the conflict that immediately preceded this period lasted for almost fifteen years. However, these ten years of piracy would be so influential that they would ingrain pirates as an unmistakable staple of culture at large. Both the men and women of this period would become the stuff of legends, largely because of the number of written works that covered the topic of piracy, the vast majority of which were romantic in nature—be they lauding or critical of the practice. This was the proper period of black flags, excessive drinking, and fighting the power in the most literal sense. Furthermore, it's also the period where piracy became a stated goal for many and, while not as prevalent as the romantic proponents of piracy would like to suggest, a preferred way of life that put freedom front and center.

Benjamin Hornigold

English by birth, Benjamin Hornigold became a privateer at an early age, but he slipped into full-on privacy in late 1713 when he was about thirty-three years old. Hornigold was an instrumental figure in forming what was later called the Pirate Republic on the island of New Providence. At the time, the island was almost exclusively inhabited by pirates and ex-privateers who came there throughout the duration of Queen Anne's War. The island was originally English, but after a few successful attacks by a French fleet in the Caribbean, most of the families who lived there, normally with no illegal activities to their name, fled, leaving New Providence and its capital, Nassau, practically empty and ripe for the taking. Pirates and privateers made the island their home, spending their time there trading stolen loot, which they spent on alcohol, prostitutes, food, and repairing their ships. And while there was no single leader on the island, the two men who influenced nearly all the other pirates there, Captains Henry Jennings and Hornigold himself, tended to have the last say in many matters due to how powerful they were.

And Hornigold was, indeed, powerful. During his time at sea, he had commanded a small fleet of five ships at one point, with around 350 men in total, adding more ships and men to his crew after each successful raid. Some sources suggest that Hornigold, unlike most pirates, was usually considerate toward his prisoners, rarely (if ever) killing them. He also maintained a strict rule of not going after English ships, possibly to maintain his status as a privateer and not an outright pirate. These particular details of his personality were responsible for his crew mutinying and voting him out as captain in 1716.

But the fascinating story of Hornigold does not end there. A few years after his crew kicked him out, Hornigold learned that a new governor of the Bahamas, Woodes Rogers, was providing royal pardons issued by King George I to all pirates who were willing to accept them. The royal pardon of 1717 offered a clean slate and the erasure of one's criminal record, while the updated pardon of 1718 also provided a cash prize to all of the ex-pirates who helped quell piracy in the region. The capture of each captain was worth £100, and £40 was offered for each captured boatswain and lieutenant. Hornigold took the opportunity and acquired a pardon from Rogers, who wisely and prudently employed Hornigold to hunt down other pirates. Hornigold did not manage to capture some of the biggest names, but he did capture a large number of pirates, some of whom were his own. Merely a year after the issuing of the royal pardon, Benjamin Hornigold would meet his end when his ship wrecked on an uncharted reef.

In terms of both piracy and pirate hunting, Hornigold was an expert with years of experience, despite dying at the age of thirty-nine. However, Hornigold is perhaps more famous for all of the other pirates he "tutored" in his early days, a few of whom we will talk about below.

Charles Vane

As we saw with François L'Olonnais and Roche Braziliano, cruelty and viciousness were not unheard of among the early buccaneers of the Golden Age. However, it was the exception, not the rule. More often than not, pirates avoided battle if they could help it, and though pirate captains were in charge of looting and sacking vessels, they rarely committed brutal acts. In fact, quite a few pirates were renowned for their decent behavior toward their crew and captives (their treatment of slaves was, at best, spotty but also not entirely cruel). During the last decade or so of the Golden Age, pirates who acted like L'Olonnais and Braziliano were sparsely found in the Caribbean, with one very notable exception, that of Charles Vane.

Vane, a native Englishman, was an active pirate under the command of Henry Jennings, one of the influential people of the so-called Pirate Republic and a rival of sorts to Benjamin Hornigold. Jennings's crew specialized in attacking ships that would come to salvage the goods of sunken Spanish galleons. It was here that Vane distinguished himself enough to captain his own ship in 1717. He was already starting to build his reputation by torturing the captives of his many raids, of which his crew did not approve. Some sources also suggest that he was just as vicious with his own men, a practice that was also freakishly uncommon among the Golden Age pirates.

Vane was one of those pirates who took pride in his craft to the point where he rejected a royal pardon twice. The first time was when King George I of England extended his offer to pardon all pirates in early 1718, at which point Vane's sloop was captured by an English naval captain named Vincent Pearse; Vane would initially accept the pardon after being captured, especially considering that several other pirates, including Hornigold, urged Pearse to release the cruel seafarer. However, Vane would not turn his back on piracy that easily. In March of the same year, he set sail with his crew, which included future prominent pirate captains like Edward England and Jack Rackham. By June, he had regained his notoriety; he took several ships and added them to his fleet, including a sizable French vessel with twenty guns.

His second refusal of a pardon came when his fleet came face to face with the ships of Woodes Rogers. Vane decided to set fire to his French ship and send it straight for Rogers's fleet. The governor's ships, save for one, took next to no damage from the fireship, but Vane did manage to escape, and he fired a few shots at Rogers's ships in the process.

Vane remained active throughout the summer of 1718. At one point, Hornigold was sent to capture him but failed to do so. In the meantime, Vane moved to the coast of the two Carolinas, at one point entering and blockading Charleston Port, making that the second time the port had been blockaded by a prominent pirate. The governor of South Carolina then commissioned a couple of armed ships to go after Vane, with one of those ships being commanded by Colonel William Rhett, a man who would never capture Vane but who would run into a different infamous pirate along the way. Vane made his way to Ocracoke Inlet (modern-day Outer Banks, North Carolina) and spent a few weeks reveling with the other pirate who had blockaded Charleston Port, with the two separating early the next morning.

Vane's fortunes were not good after this evening of revelry. In late November of 1718, his ship attacked a French frigate, and once Vane figured out just how well equipped the ship was, he ordered a tactical retreat. His men, who had already been mutinous once before, saw this as an act of cowardice. Soon enough, Vane was voted out as captain, with Jack Rackham taking over. Vane and a few of his accomplices were ditched, with his former crew leaving them in a small sloop. The former captain managed to scrape by, going after several small sloops in the region, but in February of 1719, his already tiny remaining crew was caught in a hurricane in the Bay of Honduras, which killed nearly everyone on board except for Vane and another pirate. The two managed to survive for a few months on an uninhabited island before they were rescued. Unfortunately for Vane, a man, one Captain Holford, recognized him from the days when he was in Vane's service. After telling Vane's crew everything about their past, Vane was arrested and taken to Port Royal.

Thanks to the testimony of his former compatriots, Vane's trial was short and predictable. And so, on March 22nd, 1721, Charles Vane hung for his crimes. His body was hung in chains at Gun Cay, an island in the Bahamas, as a warning to other pirates that their crimes would not pay.

Edward Teach (Blackbeard)

If there was ever an epitome of piracy, it would undoubtedly be the single most popular sea brigand in history, the man who would become the very synonym of the word "pirate": the dark-haired, tall, broad-shouldered English gentleman, Edward Teach, better known as Blackbeard. Despite only being a pirate for a year and a half, he managed to become a legend even in his own time. The first third of the Golden Age had Henry Morgan, and the second had Henry Every. But the third period of this tumultuous era unquestioningly produced the most recognizable pirate ever.

Very little is known about Teach's life, which is common for most pirate captains. Based on what was found in the wreckage of his famed ship, the aptly called *Queen Anne's Revenge*, Teach was probably a member of the nobility, as he was literate and intelligent, and he was likely born in Bristol. He was in his thirties when he reached the Caribbean, and he acted as a privateer during Queen Anne's War. Of course, after the treaty, he and his colleagues were left without a job, so he began a career in piracy, acting as one of Benjamin Hornigold's crewmen. During his time with Hornigold, Teach distinguished himself so much that he became a captain of his own sloop, and soon enough, the two men would meet another pirate, Stede Bonnet, and add his own ship to the fleet. In 1716, Hornigold was voted out as a captain, and Teach would take over the title, one that he would keep until his final breath.

The early days of Teach's piracy were incredibly successful. He managed to capture a French ship called *La Concorde* in November of 1717, a vessel that was once called *La Concorde* and that belonged to the English before being captured by the French in 1711. In other words, renaming the ship *Queen Anne's Revenge* was intentional, and neither was the fact that the French sailors renamed a ship they received in the tradeoff for *La Concorde* as *Mauvaise Rencontre* ("Bad Meeting"). Between 1717 and 1718, Teach captured a decent number of ships, plundering every vessel be it French, English, Dutch, or Spanish. One such ship was the merchant sloop *Margaret*, which was captained by one Henry Bostock. According to Bostock's later account given to Governor Walter Hamilton, Teach would be described as a "tall spare man with a very black beard which he wore very long." This was the first-ever instance of those words being mentioned in relation to Teach. Soon enough, the most famous pirate nickname ever, Blackbeard, became prominent, as did the black-bearded pirate himself.

Teach was a master strategist, both when it came to attacking his targets and handling his crew. There are somewhat exaggerated accounts of him sticking long fuses under his thick black hair and beard, then setting them on fire so that his enemies would be under the impression that hellfire itself was burning behind him. Furthermore, he supposedly wore two holsters with three rows of pistols, meaning he was always ready for action and a dangerous man to trifle with. As stated, we can't be sure of the truthfulness of these accounts, but the gist of them remains extremely likely—Teach used fear as an effective tool to keep his crew in line. This tactic also helped him retain his position as captain, considering that even the worst captains could end up being replaced by the crew, as we saw with Charles Vane.

By far, Edward Teach's greatest claim to fame was his infamous blockade of Charleston Port in late May of 1718, the same town that Vane would blockade mere months later. After entering with his fleet, Teach would capture every single ship that tried to pass the Charles Town Bar, ransack them, and relieve them of their valuables. Charleston was an important port for the English American colonies, and the blockade was a lot more than a pirate harassing entering ships; it effectively crippled the economy of the British Empire. Interestingly, Teach required nothing from the town other than medical supplies for his crew, and he threatened to execute the captured hostages from the ships he ransacked if the local governance did not comply. Of course, Teach got away with all of these crimes due to bribing the right people in the town and intimidating the rest.

After leaving Charleston, Blackbeard learned of Woodes Rogers and the pardons he gave to pirates. Both Teach and Bonnet, albeit at different times, went to a town named Bath and received a pardon from North Carolina's governor, Charles Eden, who was known for collaborating with Teach in the past. In October of 1718, Teach, now with a privateering letter of marque, would return to piracy, going to Ocracoke Inlet to spend most of his time. Ocracoke was his favorite spot to visit, and some historians speculate that he even had plans to make it a new pirate hub, one similar to Nassau or Port Royal. And considering he would enjoy a week of drinking and reveling with Charles Vane and other soon-to-be-prominent pirates (Jack Rackham being among them) there, such a hypothesis is not entirely implausible.

Teach's recent activities raised a few eyebrows among the American governors, in particular one governor named Alexander Spotswood of Virginia. After a lengthy and complex campaign, Spotswood finally managed to secure the means of capturing Blackbeard; he had two ships, HMS *Pearl* and HMS *Lyme*, which were captained by George Gordon and Ellis Brand, respectively. The two ships, however, were too big to navigate in the waters around Ocracoke, so the crews had to take two small sloops instead. The command of both was given to Gordon's lieutenant, an experienced naval officer named Robert Maynard.

Maynard was a professional soldier with years of experience and skills, and he had a military-like demeanor. In the early morning of November 22nd, his two sloops advanced on Teach, whose own ships started moving. The vessels exchanged fire, and one of Maynard's sloops was so badly damaged that it was instantly out of commission. At least a third of Maynard's men died in the attack. However, soon enough, Teach's ship, *Adventure* (*Queen Anne's Revenge* had been done away with months ago), ran onto a sandbar, effectively leaving Teach grounded. He and his men waited for an attack, which came as soon as Maynard's crew managed to get their own ship off a sandbar and into the water. Reportedly, before the ships ran atop the sandbar, Teach howled over the deck at Maynard's crew, promising he would give them no quarter. Maynard's famously brief and concise notes of the event do mention something similar taking place.

Cleverly, Maynard ordered most of his remaining crew to hide under the deck, with only himself and several others left on board. Blackbeard's men fired at the ship as it approached, and as soon as they saw the smoke clearing, they boarded the ship with guns and blades out. However, Maynard's remaining crew jumped out, and the success of the surprise attack was all but guaranteed. Teach's undisciplined pirates did manage to put up a fight against trained, professional men of the English navy, but it was not to last.

During the chaos, Maynard and Teach locked eyes and engaged in what is possibly the single greatest duel involving a pirate during the Golden Age. Of course, both men did so strategically; Maynard was significantly shorter than Teach, and going against Blackbeard head-on and beating him would have a powerful psychological effect on the pirate captain's crew. On the other hand, Blackbeard beating the commander of the two English vessels would be the best possible rallying point for his men. The two seafarers first shot their pistols at each other, with Blackbeard missing and Maynard hitting his opponent with a non-lethal strike. The men then exchanged several blows with their swords, and Blackbeard supposedly broke Maynard's sword in the process. However, Maynard's crew would soon surround the duelers, and they would either shoot or slash at the pirate captain, inflicting plenty of injuries. Maynard was getting ready to shoot Teach again, and the pirate wanted to use this opportunity to lunge at Maynard and kill him. However, one of Maynard's crew, supposedly a Scottish Highlander by birth, sliced the back of Teach's neck with a broadsword, injuring him badly. Moments later, another blow from the Highlander decapitated the pirate captain, and in a millisecond, Edward Teach's lifeless body fell onto the ground. His surviving pirates were either killed in action or taken prisoner. The whole fight lasted, at most, around ten minutes.

Maynard's inspection of Teach's body revealed that the pirate was shot at least five times and cut at least twenty times, not counting the decapitation. Maynard took Blackbeard's head with him as proof of his mission, and he tossed the captain's body overboard. His crew took about £90 each from Blackbeard's booty, which goes some way in explaining why no award (which was offered to any man who managed to apprehend or kill Blackbeard) was given to him for four years. And though he would eventually get several promotions, Maynard faded into obscurity, dying peacefully at the age of sixty-six in Kent.

Many details about Blackbeard were left out of this section, mainly because few of them can actually be verified as accurate. In fact, on the face of it, it's a miracle that someone like Blackbeard managed to become such a feared and remembered pirate, especially if we consider the bizarre fact that he had, at least according to contemporary reports, never killed a single person during his time as a pirate. Nevertheless, his life remains a fascinating tale of a man who used fear and intimidation as accurately as he used a pistol and blade to become one of the most notorious sea brigands that the world has ever seen. Nearly every single stereotypical image of a pirate somehow mimics him and his antics.

The capture of Blackbeard (center left, fighting Lieutenant Maynard), a modern artistic rendition by Jean Leon Gerome Ferris, 1920

Stede Bonnet

Stede Bonnet was a prominent pirate captain who had encounters with heavyweights like Blackbeard, Vane, and Rackham, and he would, in fact, be the pirate whom William Rhett captured on route to locating Vane. However, none of these facts make Stede Bonnet a fascinating figure. This man, known to his contemporaries as the "Gentleman Pirate," became famous (or rather infamous) because of his sheer incompetence and bizarre sets of circumstances. Namely, he was someone who had willingly left a cozy, comfortable, well-to-do life of a wealthy landowner, bought a ship, hired a crew, and willingly became a pirate, a decision that was indeed unique and incredibly mind-boggling, even to his contemporaries. In a sense, he was the first real fan of the concept of piracy, and he took his admiration for the practice a step too far.

When Bonnet was close to turning thirty, he was the owner of a large estate near Bridgetown in Barbados. He inherited this land after his father's death in 1694, and a few years later, he would marry a woman by the name of Mary Allamby, who went on to give birth to his three sons and a daughter. He wasn't entirely without experience in fighting, as he served as a member of the Barbados militia and earned the rank of major. But in terms of sailing, he knew next to nothing. In early 1717, for reasons that are still not completely known to history, Bonnet bought a large ship, named it *Revenge*, and staffed it with seventy experienced pirates. Unlike other pirate captains, he did not capture his ship in a battle or gain it through mutiny, and furthermore, he and his men did not earn massive loot from plunders at first. He instead came to the mind-boggling decision to pay his pirates regular wages as if they were his employees.

Considering his lack of knowledge on everything sea-related, he relied on the advice of his quartermaster and officer. The rest of the crew showed no respect for Bonnet, often openly mocking him for his actions. Nevertheless, his ship managed to capture and raid several decent targets in the coming months, possibly thanks to Bonnet's experienced officers more than himself. In late 1717, however, Bonnet would be badly wounded after a skirmish with a Spanish man-of-war (a powerful frigate used by navy officers during maritime battles), and he would make his way to Nassau for much-needed repairs and to replace his crew, as half of them died in the fight against the Spanish.

Bonnet would meet Blackbeard on Nassau, and the two men decided to cooperate. During their sailing endeavors, Teach was effectively in charge of Bonnet's ship. The Gentleman Pirate was unable to give any orders, which only prompted his crew to mock him more. However, we can reasonably assume that Teach had a soft spot for Bonnet, as he kept Bonnet around the ship and did not kill or maroon him somewhere along the way. Perhaps Teach did this out of sheer pity. After the infamous Charlestown blockade, Teach confided in Bonnet that he wanted to take the king's pardon, a decision with which Bonnet would come to agree and proceeded to do so himself. He received his pardon from Charles Eden, along with permission to go to the island of St. Thomas and obtain a letter of marque, which would enable him to work as a privateer against Spanish ships.

Of course, Bonnet couldn't resist pirating, so after adopting an alias and renaming his ship, he went back to plundering small vessels around the Caribbean and the American coast. Over the months, he actually became somewhat proficient in this practice, at least enough to regain some of his old notoriety. In the summer of 1718, Colonel William Rhett would be sent on his mission to capture Charles Vane and other notorious pirates, and his two ships would eventually run into Bonnet on October 3rd, who was stationed at Cape Fear River (modern-day North Carolina), waiting out the upcoming Atlantic hurricanes. A long, protracted battle ensued between Rhett and Bonnet, with the Gentleman Pirate's men holding their ground at first. However, Rhett would eventually triumph, and he arrested Bonnet then and there.

Bonnet was taken to Charleston, where he was imprisoned. Soon after, on October 24th, he managed to escape with another fellow pirate, but he was soon recaptured and sent right back behind bars. The court ruled him guilty, but Bonnet pleaded with South Carolina's governor, Robert Johnson, for clemency. At one point, Bonnet even suggested that Johnson cut his own arms and legs so he could never be physically able to go pirating again. Supposedly, this little outburst convinced the governor that Bonnet was of an insane mind, so the execution was delayed until December 10th. Bonnet met his demise on that day by hanging.

The story of Stede Bonnet is far from a typical pirate yarn. Some of his decisions and motives still baffle historians today, and they question everything from his intelligence and self-awareness to his reasoning. If anything, his story clearly shows us that anyone back in the day could be a pirate, especially people who clearly don't belong in that group.

Howell Davis

Howell Davis's career as a pirate was not particularly long, lasting just short of a year (he was active between July 18th, 1718, and June 19th, 1719). However, during those eleven months, this Welsh gentleman left an impression on his contemporaries as a cunning, shrewd, intelligent, and even somewhat noble pirate.

Initially a mate on a slave ship, Davis would become a captive, then a recruit, of famed pirate captain Edward England. There are indications that Davis willingly chose a life of piracy due to England's own character as a captain, as he vehemently refused to kill captives and treated the people he raided humanely. Davis was in control of the same slave ship he had been on when he joined England's crew, but the pirates on board were not thrilled with how

Davis commanded, so they mutinied and took his ship to Barbados, where Davis would be arrested. Astoundingly, he was released after just three months, which almost never happened with captured outspoken pirates. Governors of the region, including Woodes Rogers himself, were notorious for almost always sentencing pirates to death, so historians speculate that Davis's charm and charisma must have somehow worked in his favor. Davis wanted to reach New Providence next, but after learning of Rogers's anti-pirate stance, he instead went the other direction. He reached Martinique, and with the help of six other sailors, he mutinied and took control of the ship after being elected captain once more. He chose Coxen Hole (in modern-day Honduras on the island of Roatán) as his base, which was no accident; the spot itself was named after a French buccaneer, Captain John Coxen, and the island it was on used to house over five thousand pirates during the early period of the Golden Age. From this base, Davis conducted several successful raids before settling on a new target: the West African coast.

Davis tried avoiding fighting as much as possible, instead resorting to completely different means of depriving ships and settlements of their wealth. For example, when he reached the Cape Verde islands off the coast of Africa, he began to dress like a dandy and posed as an English privateer, tricking the local governor into letting him pass. At one point, while still in disguise, Davis entered a Royal African fort on the Gambia River and tricked the local Portuguese governor into inviting him over. Davis proceeded to keep the man hostage and released him only after taking £2,000 as compensation. His West African raid campaign saw him team up with two other pirates: French Captain Olivier La Bouche and the English brigand Thomas Cocklyn. Together, they raided a slave ship called *Bird Galley* at the mouth of the Sierra Leone River, later releasing its captain, William Snelgrave, with a small sloop and some meager supplies. Snelgrave's account of Davis actually lets us know just how influential and charismatic he had been. Apparently, it was Cocklyn who originally captured the *Bird Galley*, but he was extremely hostile to the captured crew and even tortured them. Davis intervened; he confronted Cocklyn and made sure the prisoners were treated well. This behavior and the captain's charm left a huge impression on Snelgrave, who was noted as saying that Davis, despite the profession he had been in, was a generous and humane man.

Davis continued to raid the African coast, eventually capturing a ship with a fellow Welshman who begrudgingly joined Davis's crew, one Bartholomew Roberts. However, at one point, Davis bit off more than he could chew. In mid-June, he came to the island of Principe while posing as a pirate hunter. He captured a French vessel along the way with a shoddy claim that it housed pirates wanting to raid the island's fort. He was on his way to speak to the local Portuguese governor in an attempt to kidnap him and hold him for ransom. However, somehow, the governor's guards found out about his plan and ambushed Davis. He was killed on the spot, with his crew taking revenge for his death not long after.

By all accounts, Davis was a respected man and one of those rare pirates who actually had a lot of natural charisma. In fact, few pirate captains would inspire such loyalty for their crew to avenge them after death. But Davis's crew would do just that, and they would go on to commit more acts of piracy, this time under a captain that would prove to be a much more prominent, famous, and intimidating pirate than Davis.

Calico Jack Rackham

For fans of the *Pirates of the Caribbean* franchise, Captain Jack Sparrow (played by Johnny Depp) might seem a tad excessive, with his exaggerated moves, staggering walk, mumbling language, and eccentric sense of fashion. But like all fictional pirates, Sparrow's character draws inspiration from several real-world sources. One of those would be Howell Davis due to his charisma and sense of flair. However, the more prominent inspiration for Sparrow was undoubtedly a man who was born as John or Jack Rackham. He would bear the nickname Calico Jack.

Rackham, called Calico Jack due to his choice of wearing calico clothing (calico is a type of coarse fabric made from unprocessed cotton), was an Englishman who, at first, served as Charles Vane's quartermaster until the mutiny of 1718. After taking over Vane's ship, Rackham made a career of capturing small fishing vessels and intimidating the locals, never straying too far from the coastline. By all intents and purposes, Rackham was not a notorious, noteworthy pirate captain who would have been remembered, unlike his more famous colleagues (including his former captain). Though he would capture a few larger ships, he remained a small-time criminal up until 1719 when he asked Woodes Rogers for a royal pardon. Rackham would receive this pardon, but it would not stop him from pirating.

After receiving the document from Rogers, Rackham sailed to Nassau and spent most of his time with other pirates, plotting, scheming, and drinking the days away. Once there, he met and got involved with a woman by the name of Anne Bonny, and the two began a love affair. Since Bonny was married at the time, the affair caused a scandal, which prompted the couple to sail away from Nassau. Rackham resumed pirating, with Bonny now a member of his crew. Of course, he reverted to attacking small fishing boats and merchant ships, and he captured and recruited more members along the way, including yet another female pirate, Mary Read.

Rackham's activities became well known in the region, and Rogers, knowing that Calico Jack had broken the terms of his pardon, sent two pirate hunters after him, those being Captain Jonathan Barnet and former pirate Jean Bonadvis. The two men managed to locate Rackham's ship on the Jamaican coast. A battle ensued, with the pirate hunters severely damaging Rackham's ship and the pirate crew asking for quarter. Everyone was arrested and brought to Spanish Town, Jamaica, in November of 1720 for their trial.

It was this trial that actually made Rackham famous and "saved" him from being just another footnote in history. Both Bonny and Read managed to escape hanging by claiming that they were pregnant, which astounded both the jurors and the general public. Female pirates were extremely rare, yet Rackham somehow had two women among his crew—to call this situation sensational would be a massive understatement. The women were not sentenced, but Jack and most of his crew faced the gallows. Rackham himself was hung for his crimes on November 19th, with his body being coated in tar and hung on a gibbet on an island just outside Port Royal. The island is now morbidly called Rackham's Cay in honor of his execution.

Rackham's set of circumstances made him a "household name" among both fans of piracy and their fiercest opponents, despite him only preying on local ships that had little real value. He was far from a competent captain, having made many mistakes throughout his career, but the mere fact that his crew was so unorthodox and that he was hunted by some of the most prominent men of that age goes to show that anything in life is possible.

Anne Bonny

As stated earlier, female pirates were incredibly rare during the Golden Age of Piracy. There are multiple reasons behind this, not least of which was the harsh and deadly life of a pirate. Furthermore, pirates were known to deal in some disturbing criminal activity, which included rape. So, having a woman on board a ship surrounded by men out at sea was dangerous, to say the least. In addition, pirates would fight amongst themselves for the affection of a woman on deck, which would bring about discord and result in severe consequences. However, that still did not prevent some women from becoming pirates. In fact, nearly two centuries before the third segment of the Golden Age period, one of the most notorious pirate captains was an Irish noblewoman called Grace O'Malley, whose exploits became the stuff of legends.

Interestingly enough, the two prominent female pirates of the Golden Age would be part of the same crew under the same captain, and they, most likely, would end up in a sexual relationship with him. Also, it should be noted that neither of these women was a captain of her own ship. They were both regular crew members serving under the same man.

One of those women was Anne Bonny, a red-haired firebrand who was most likely born somewhere in Ireland. Her entire life prior to meeting Jack Rackham is unknown and left to speculation, and the only source that references it is full of fancy and exaggeration. What we do know is that prior to meeting Rackham on Nassau, she was already married and had a reputation as being an independent go-getter and a bit of a tomboy. Some sources claim that Rackham insisted she divorce her husband, but it never happened, so the two simply escaped at sea. At that point, she became a full member of his crew.

Contrary to popular belief, neither Bonny nor her other female associate, Mary Read, wore male clothes aboard Rackham's ship, though Read did wear male uniforms early in her piratical career. It should be noted that the practice of women dressing as boys or men to join the navy was not unheard of, as uncommon as it may have been.

At some point, Rackham's crew picked up new crew members from a ransacked ship, a disguised Mary Read among them. Bonny apparently took a fancy to Read, but when they both exposed themselves to each other, they remained friends. Jack did not enjoy Bonny's flirtatious side; despite that, the two remained a couple, with Bonny even giving birth to his child. Before she did, Rackham sailed to Cuba and left her there so that the birth could happen without problems. Not long after she gave birth, though, Bonny got right back at sea and rejoined Rackham in his exploits.

During the trial after their capture, both Bonny and Read pleaded with the court, claiming that they were pregnant. According to law, pregnant women were not to be executed. Killing a pregnant woman, even one who was sentenced to death, was considered a grave sin in England, so authorities either waited for the woman to give birth and then dispatch her or expose her as a fraud for lying about her pregnancy, which also resulted in death. We will likely never know what happened to Anne Bonny, as all sources stay silent on her fate after the trial.

Anne Bonny, engraving from the Dutch edition of Captain Charles Johnson's A General History of the Pyrates, 18ᵗʰ Century

Mary Read

A native of London, Mary Read was the second woman on Rackham's ship, and she was the only one of the two who actually had a bit of a cross-dressing military career behind her. While she was still young, she wore boy's clothes and enlisted in the army as a foot soldier, soon earning a cavalry rank after her bravery during either the Nine Years' War or the War of the Spanish Succession. It was apparently around this time that she fell in love with a

Flemish soldier. She exposed her sex to him at some point, which prompted the two to get married. They acquired an inn near Breda Castle in the Netherlands called The Three Horseshoes (*De Drie Hoefijzers*) and ran it until her husband's early death. Devastated, Read once again wore male clothes and went back into service.

Back at sea, Read joined a privateering vessel on its way to the Spanish Main, but the vessel would be attacked and ransacked by none other than Jack Rackham. Read joined his crew, and Bonny, mistaking Read for a man, took an instant interest in her. Once they revealed who they were to each other, the two women continued working alongside Rackham, at times proving to be even fiercer than his male pirates. One account at the time described them as brash, loud, and just as prone to cussing as the male pirates. Apparently, the women had no trouble ordering other pirates to murder the captive women on board.

Read evidently showed a lot of bravery and savagery during the final battle between Rackham's crew and Barnet's men, as she supposedly shot in the crowd of unready pirates and berated them for their cowardice. Once the crew had been captured and taken to court, both Bonny and Read pleaded with the court not to sentence them to death due to their pregnancies. However, of the two women, it was evident only Read was actually with child; she had conceived it with a crew member on Rackham's ship. Sadly, unlike Bonny, we know exactly what happened to Read. She contracted a severe fever while in the dungeon and died not long after, with her child probably also dying while still in the womb.

Interestingly, Bonny and Read would prove to be somewhat contradictory in their bearing. For example, Bonny behaved like a brutish tomboy and a free spirit, despite looking incredibly feminine and actually bearing a child first. On the other hand, Read was a lot more feminine in behavior—she actually wanted to fall in love, bear children, and live as a common housewife—yet she dressed as a man and had a more manly demeanor to her actions than Bonny.

John Taylor

Like Every and Bonny before him, John Taylor was another pirate whose ultimate fate is unknown. However, what we do know is that his life as a pirate was full of success after success, with two of the biggest pirate plunders involving him in a huge capacity, either as a quartermaster to Edward England or as a captain in his own right.

Taylor showed a lot of promise as a pirate while under England's control. Unlike most pirates during the last decade of the Golden Age, Taylor actually operated in what used to be the haven of the Pirate Round, i.e., Madagascar and its surrounding waters. He started off as one of the men aboard the *Buck*, the same ship Howell Davis would take over during his mutiny. Taylor actually tried to overthrow Davis, but he ultimately left and joined a few different crews, befriending Olivier La Bouche and Thomas Cocklyn and raiding around Madagascar before joining England's fleet. England's ship *Fancy* and the deceased Cocklyn's ship *Victory* sailed side by side in an attempt to take a massive prize: the English East India Company's *Cassandra*. The ship's captain, James Macrae, put up a strong resistance, but after the pirates more or less devastated his ship, he and some of his crew retreated to the forest close to the shore. Macrae, to his credit, came back by himself to face the pirates, who were looting en masse from the damaged *Cassandra*, and he negotiated a ransom for his ship. England admired Macrae's boldness, and he was soon given a small ship and half of his old cargo to return safely to India.

However, Taylor and a large number of England's crew were livid at this decision for two reasons. Firstly, a huge portion of the booty went back to the man they had just raided. Secondly, and more importantly, Macrae had been responsible for killing more than a few crew members of both England and Taylor, and that was unacceptable. Once they were back at sea, Taylor gathered enough people to vote England as unfit to lead, and they made him leave the ship on a small boat. Taylor was now in command, being on board *Cassandra* with La Bouche and another famed pirate, Jasper Seagar, as his allies. In December 1720, the pirates, after a successful season of raiding and robbing, stopped off at Madagascar to trade with a man who would become an incredibly prominent name in Malagasy history, a pirate trader called James Plantain. It seemed like Taylor was on a winning streak, but his victories were nothing compared to what happened in April of the very next year.

Taylor, Seagar, and La Bouche sailed to Reunion Island (today a French overseas territory near Madagascar), where a massive prize waited for them. It was none other than the huge seven-hundred-ton treasure-heavy vessel called *Nossa Senhora do Cabo* ("Our Lady of the Cape"), and it was relatively easy to capture since it had lost its mast in a storm. And the loot was incredibly bountiful—the three pirates escaped with gold, jewels, and church regalia that had a combined worth of one million pounds. Furthermore, the pirates also took *Nossa Senhora do Cabo* as part of their fleet.

Seagar would die soon after the raid while the three were in Madagascar, with the British Royal Navy now hot on their trail. Taylor and La Bouche each took a ship (Taylor chose *Cassandra*), and they went their separate ways, with the English pirate going to the West Indies. He reached his destination in 1723, and he visited Portobello and asked for a pardon from the Spanish governor there. Taylor received one, becoming a member of the Armada de Barlovento (the same one that Laurens de Graaf had humiliated decades before). He was tasked to hunt for logwood cutters around the Caribbean. That was the last time Taylor was mentioned in historical documents, with his future exploits and even the date of his death left for speculation.

Bartholomew Roberts (Black Bart)

In terms of popularity, Black Bart was almost as well known as Blackbeard and Every, and in terms of brutality, he was nowhere near Vane or L'Olonnais. However, he would go down in history as probably the most successful pirate, as he captured up to 470 ships in his lifetime. Granted, most of those ships were small sloops and fishing boats, but the number still stands as a highlight of his career, and it would merely be one of many details that made Black Bart a staple of pirate culture.

Bartholomew Roberts was born in Wales, with his birth name actually being John. He had been a sailor since he was thirteen years old, and as fate would have it, a ship he was on would end up being boarded by pirates, with Howell Davis at the helm. Davis took an instant liking to Roberts, and though he was extremely reluctant to do so, the Welshman joined Davis's crew.

The night Davis was killed by the men of the governor of Principe, his crew swore vengeance. The best man possible to lead them in this endeavor was the only other Welshman on board: the moody, brooding, and cold Roberts. As captain, his first order of business was to go after the governor. Under cover of night, the men sailed to the island, killed most of the governor's men, and took off with plenty of looted valuables. After a few successful seizures of ships, the crewmen found themselves in Brazil. It would be between 1719 and 1720, the first year of Roberts's captaincy, that they would capture their first major prize. As they were on the Brazilian coast, they spotted a fleet of forty-two armed Portuguese ships, with the richest and the biggest being *Sagrada Familia*. Despite being outnumbered, Roberts and his men actually captured the ship and escaped with it to the Caribbean. Not long after, he would capture a brigantine near the Surinam River, but while he was busy capturing it, the man left in charge of Black Bart's main ship, Walter Kennedy, sailed away. Enraged, Roberts vowed vengeance upon Kennedy. He renamed the new ship *Fortune*, and with overwhelming agreement from his crew members, he drafted a set of rules that would be just one of many examples of a so-called pirate code.

Ships from both Barbados and Martinique were sent after Roberts while he was sailing in the Caribbean, with the ones from Barbados actually crippling his fleet and forcing the captain to take his ship somewhere for repairs (it also caused many deaths as well, with at least twenty of Roberts's men dying from wounds obtained in the skirmish). It was at this time that Roberts supposedly commissioned a new black flag to be made for him. On this flag, Bart himself stood on top of two skulls, with "ABH" and "AMH" written under each skull. The first acronym stood for "A Barbadian Head" and the other for "A Martinique Head," underlying his hatred for the two islands and his desire for vengeance.

Between June 1720 and April 1721, Black Bart and his crew sailed in the waters around Newfoundland and the Caribbean. This period was extremely prolific for Roberts. In a single outing, on June 21st, while he and his crew were in an abandoned Trepassey harbor in Newfoundland, he spotted 22 merchant ships and 150 small fishing boats. He captured all twenty-two ships, and once the time came, he burned all the rest and sailed away. During this period of ten months, he managed to capture several ships around Cape Breton, a dozen vessels in the Ferryland harbor, nine French ships after leaving Trepassey, a fairly large number of vessels before reaching the West Indies, several more ships in Basse Terra Road (a roadstead) near St. Christopher's Island, fifteen ships near Saint Lucia, and possibly even a ship owned by the contemporary governor of Martinique. That's several hundreds of ships in under a year, and it was only the beginning.

Roberts next set sail for West Africa, and the following eight months saw him raiding and claiming more ships. In early June, he captured two French ships near the mouth of the Senegal River. Next, he moved to Sierra Leone, as he had learned about the Royal Navy ships that had left the region. One of those ships, the HMS *Swallow*, would be a key element in the events that occurred during Roberts's final days. Cestos Point in Liberia was Roberts's next stop, and there, he captured two large ships. By January of next year, he had taken about a dozen more ships before entering Ouidah (in modern-day Benin). Immediately upon entry, he took control of several more ships, releasing them quickly after and receiving a ransom for them. Despite his propensity for capturing ships, Roberts only had three vessels when he was operating around the African coast: the *Royal Fortune* (one of several, as this was Roberts's favorite ship name), the *Ranger*, and the *Little Ranger*. They were all careened on Cape Lopez in modern-day Gabon.

Roberts even managed to capture another ship a mere day before his demise, with the crews of both ships drinking themselves into a stupor before the navy arrived on February 5th. The HMS *Swallow* tactically picked them off one by one, and during the final battle against the *Royal Fortune*, Black Bart wore his finest clothes and was on deck giving orders. A single grapeshot from the HMS *Swallow*'s cannon hit Roberts directly, killing him in an instant. His followers fought a protracted battle and eventually lost, with the navy arresting them and taking them elsewhere for trial. Most of his crew were executed, with the black members (all former slaves) being sold back into slavery. However, a number of people managed to survive their trial.

Roberts was a fascinating figure for several reasons. Not only was he an effective navigator and a skilled seafarer, but he was also a man who spoke his mind and rarely gave up. Sources also claim that he drank very little beer and that he abstained from sex completely, devoting himself to the task at hand instead. Of course, he did not prevent his own men from drinking, but he did have strict rules about other acts. His pirate code, in particular, gives us a glimpse of what the atmosphere on a pirate ship was like, as well as an idea of what constituted a crime or a breach of trust among pirates. Furthermore, Roberts was also a flamboyant dresser, at least according to some sources. His preference for red coats and big shiny crosses speaks of a desire to stand out and maintain his position among his men. However, it also speaks of his religious leanings, as Roberts was a devout Christian. Finally, despite his clear apprehension for many piratical practices, his supposed famous quote sums up how a pirate captain might have felt during the Golden Age of Piracy:

"In an honest service there is thin commons, low wages, and hard labor; in this, plenty and satiety, pleasure and ease, liberty and power; and who would not balance creditor on this side, when all the hazard that is run for it, at worst, is only a sour look or two at choking. No, a merry life and a short one shall be my motto."

Death of Howell Davis, from The Pirates Own Book by Charles Ellms, 1837

Abraham Samuel

Abraham Samuel's story is one that more or less started the beginning of what would be the closing chapter of the Pirate Round during the Golden Age. Much like Baldridge at Île Sainte-Marie,

Samuel would establish a base at the old French fort known as Fort Dauphin (modern-day Tôlanaro) at the southern coast of Madagascar. From there, he would dedicate his time to trading with pirates and other illicit merchants, amassing a fortune. Samuel and another pirate would usher in an interesting age in Madagascar that took place over the final decades of the Golden Age of Piracy, namely the age of the self-proclaimed pirate kings of Madagascar.

Samuel was a mixed-race man (a mulatto, i.e., of mixed Caucasian and African origin). He was originally from Martinique and served as a quartermaster on a pirate ship in the Arabian Sea in 1696. A year later, he found himself shipwrecked, along with his fellow crewmen, on the southern shore of Madagascar, and so, they set up camp at Fort Dauphin, which was abandoned at that time. In an interesting twist of fate, an elderly princess of a local Antanosy tribe (the Antanosy are a tribal group in the south of Madagascar) spotted them and singled out Samuel. She thought he was her son, who was born to a Frenchman who had abandoned her while she was young. Samuel, of course, had nothing to do with the Antanosy, nor was he really French himself, but he readily accepted this newfound label and began to see himself as the lawful heir to the Antanosy throne. By deposing the current monarch, Samuel and at least three hundred Antanosy soldiers and roughly twenty pirates took over the area around Fort Dauphin. Samuel styling himself as the "King of Port Dolfphin, Tollannare, Farrawe, Fanquestt, and Fownzahira in Madagascar."

He would frequently wage war with the surrounding Antanosy tribes, especially one king known as Diamarang Diamera. Lots of local chieftains and officials paid him tribute and served as his personal guard. In the meantime, Samuel outfitted Fort Dauphin and made it so strong and durable that it began to rival Île Sainte-Marie in strength and brilliance. From Fort Dauphin, Samuel would receive many different pirates and trade with them. Samuel's reign ended in 1705 when, as an elderly man, he went to war against a neighboring tribe and died two months later. As early as next year, a different king took over and refused to discuss what happened to Samuel with a visiting Dutch slave ship's captain.

Abraham Samuel is, at least historically speaking, one of the few non-white pirates to reach any kind of prominence during the

Golden Age; to be more precise, he was one of the few non-white pirates operating entirely within the areas where European piracy thrived. His presence at Madagascar, much like that of the pirate in the paragraphs that follow, radically shifted the local Malagasy political scales (or rather, the political scales of the many different tribal groups on the island), and his compatriots, like those of Baldridge, would frequently intermarry with the local women and produce offspring. A few would even be buried in nearby cemeteries.

James Plantain

If we count oddness and unpredictability alone, Madagascar was by far the most interesting place related to the Golden Age of Piracy. Even in its late stages, it was a prominent spot for seafarers to gather, exchange goods, revel in vice, and repair broken ships. It was also a spot where everyday men could literally declare themselves royalty and, more importantly, maintain that position with actual power and an iron hand. And while Abraham Samuel was indeed a great example of a successful "King of Madagascar," he was neither the only one to bear that title nor was he even the most successful monarch of European (and piratical) descent. That honor belongs to a young English upstart called James (or John) Plantain.

Plantain's tale is one of the most incredible globetrotting yarns about an everyday man who reached greatness and became connected to some of the most important people of the day, be they lawful or otherwise. Born in 1700, at the dawn of the War of the Spanish Succession, Plantain started his piratical career early, and soon enough, he would be part of Edward England's crew. In fact, he was present when England and his fleet went after Macrae and his ship, *Cassandra*. When John Taylor took over as captain and England was banished, Plantain joined Taylor, and the two moved to the north of Madagascar. Here, Plantain used some of the loot he had taken from the raid of *Cassandra* and rebuilt the fort at Ranter Bay in northeast Madagascar in the summer of 1720. Even though he was a mere twenty-year-old, Plantain was so charismatic and determined that the local tribes began collaborating with him, and some of the older pirates from England's former crew decided on following the young man in his quest to establish himself as an important fixture on the island. And this he did, styling himself as the "King of Ranter Bay." He would maintain his power through trade, intimidation, cunning, warfare, and even marriage.

The northeast of Madagascar was home to some colorful individuals of nobility, most notably a chieftain called Mulatto Tom, who claimed, among other things, to be the illegitimate son of Henry Every. Mulatto Tom frequently visited Plantain's fort, along with another local chieftain called King Dick. King Dick's granddaughter, a mixed-race beauty called Eleanora, became the object of Plantain's affections. He wanted to marry her, but King Dick vehemently refused the marriage. What followed was possibly one of the most interesting events in 18th-century Madagascar history. The young king of Ranter Bay, with three regiments of native warriors under the command of his two pirate compatriots— James Adair from Scotland and Hans Burgen from Denmark— attacked King Dick. King Dick's forces were formidable and, amusingly, contained multiple aged and experienced European pirates in their ranks. It was a proper multiethnic war, and Plantain emerged victorious, forcing King Dick to flee. Plantain caught up with him, and another battle ensued. Once again, King Dick was defeated. Plantain then burned his village in front of him and took Eleanora (nicknamed Holy Eleanora due to her very basic Christian upbringing), but he flew into a fit of rage when he found out that she had already been impregnated by a different pirate. King Dick felt Plantain's wrath since he was executed then and there. Plantain kept Eleanora as his wife, however, and she would go on to give birth to many of his future children.

All of these events took place in 1722 when Plantain was merely twenty-two years old. In that same year, the British Crown sent four men-of-war, under the command of the experienced Commodore Thomas Mathews, to deal with the pirates of the Pirate Round and to protect the interests of the East India Company. During the war against King Dick, Plantain received Mathews and his crew, and the two even exchanged some goods, which would later lead to Mathews losing his position as a commodore due to dealing with a pirate and neglecting his duty.

Plantain's next move was to expand his territory since he was no longer satisfied with being the (now rightful) king of Ranter Bay. In the years that followed, Plantain would take land after land, going south all the way to Fort Dauphin. The fort was now under a new, unnamed native king, as Samuel had been dead for twelve years at that point. Plantain besieged the fort for a grand total of eighteen months before its king was defeated. The pirate upstart from Jamaica had now become the proper "King of Madagascar," from north to south, and he was barely twenty-four years old.

Yet, his reign was not to last long. All of the wars must have depleted his supplies or his spirit, and he had made a lot of enemies across the island. Like most monarchs, he gave into his excesses and acted like a tyrant, though strangely, he remained somewhat loyal to Eleanora and her to him. At some point in 1728, he had a sloop built, and as soon as it was finished, he filled it with his ill-gotten riches and sailed away from Madagascar with Eleanora and his many children. At some point, he even reached India or, more specifically, the Maratha Empire, which at the time was ruled by Shahu Bhosale I. Shahu's navy had employed a large number of European seamen, and it was controlled by the skilled and powerful Admiral Kanhoji Angre. Angre immediately recognized Plantain's skills and gave him the post of chief gunner. It's at this point where history loses track of James Plantain; most historians speculate that he spent the rest of his days in India with his family.

Plantain's tale is a genuine adventure that took him in so many different directions that they could fill many novels. Not only was he a successful pirate in his early days, but he was also an incredible tactician, warrior, leader, and monarch. Furthermore, he was a skilled tradesman who managed to amass huge wealth and still maintain his position as the king of an island nation to which he had literally zero real relation. In addition, he met some of the most important people of that age, including Edward England, John Taylor, and Kanhoji Angre. And as if that weren't enough, there are two more segments of his story that are worth mentioning. First and foremost, he and his compatriots were singlehandedly responsible for a massive ethnic shift on the island, as they produced so many mixed-race offspring that an entire ethnic minority would form. A lot of them would try to claim a ruling position in local tribal politics. The second segment ties into the myths about pirates in general, as Plantain was known to bury and unearth small portions of his massive wealth whenever he needed them, in effect creating his own myth of the buried pirate treasure (which some people of Madagascar still look for to this very day with no success).

Chapter 4 – The End of the Golden Age: Woodes Rogers and the End of Prominent Pirate Captains

When we talk about the end of the Golden Age of Piracy, we have to keep in mind a few things. Firstly, the end of the Golden Age does not mean the end of piracy as a whole or even the end of piracy in the 17th century. Records from ports across the known world, from East India Company's many factories to harbors in France, England, and the Netherlands, all show that importers continued to suffer massive losses due to maritime crime, and the papers of the day continued to show a steady flow of arrests and trials of various pirates well into the 18th century and beyond. Of course, the frequency of pirate attacks in the Caribbean and around Africa did go down significantly, and few noteworthy pirate captains of renown appeared during this period. More importantly, the governments of each country started to take piracy seriously, and little by little, they began to weed it out as the Golden Age came to a close.

The second thing we need to keep in mind is that the end of this illegal enterprise was not sudden but rather came in phases. After all, if your waters are infested with thousands of pirates, and your navy has been decimated due to an entire decade of warfare, you can't exactly go all-out and take care of the problem in one fell swoop. The matter had to be taken care of delicately, and it had to be dealt with mostly by local governors, either with the king's permission or on their own accord (and at their own expense). By far, the most effective solution seemed to be simple; in order to appease the pirates, the king would issue pardons if they confessed to previous crimes, but if there were pirates who refused to comply, pirate hunters would be deployed to track them down. Furthermore, the known pirate bases such as Nassau, Port Royal, and so forth needed to have a pirate hunter who was directly in the thick of things and micromanaging the whole affair. One such individual was found and sent to Nassau, a man who was soon to be hailed as a hero by the English despite not getting nearly enough credit at the time.

Woodes Rogers

Contemporaries have described Rogers in realistic yet not unflattering terms. He was a tall, paunchy man with soft auburn hair and permanently frowning brows. His demeanor was calm and collected, and he rarely yelled or exploded in anger. Instead, he had a cold and calculating countenance everywhere he went. However, by no means did his demeanor match what he was capable of. When pushed hard enough, Rogers was able to exact some of the most draconian penalties, such as hanging eight men for simply going against their word. Nevertheless, Rogers was an honest man and a devout Christian who tried to maintain his honesty to the best of his abilities. That alone made him a good choice to deal with the pirate problem in the Caribbean, but it was by no means the only reason for his selection.

The other important reason Rogers was chosen as the next governor of the Bahamas was his experience at sea. From 1708 to 1711, Rogers circumnavigated the globe. He lost a brother in the voyage and sustained a massive injury while capturing a Spanish galleon called *Nuestra Señora de la Encarnación y Desengaño*. It was during this voyage that Rogers rescued Alexander Selkirk, a Scottish sailor who was stranded on the island of Más a Tierra for four years and whose story would inspire Daniel Defoe to write his bestselling novel, *Robinson Crusoe*. Rogers wrote of his experiences at sea in his own book, *A Cruising Voyage Round the World*, which became a bestseller.

To sum up, Rogers was not only a man of some repute with an honorable personality that a prospective governor and pirate hunter needed, but he also had lots of practical experience at sea, both as a sailor and as a privateer. Furthermore, he already enjoyed the status of a hero. But those were not the only reasons behind his employment by the English Crown. Another major reason was the fact that Rogers more or less had no choice but to do it. By the time he was back in England, Rogers had to declare bankruptcy and was going through a divorce. His crew successfully sued him for failing to pay them their proper wages during the expedition around the world, and though his book was successful, the earnings from it were far from enough to cover the costs of the lawsuit and the compensation of his former crew. After having sold his property and separating from his wife, Sarah, Rogers decided to go on another expedition in order to attain more wealth, so he made his way to Madagascar. His original mission was to purchase slaves and resell them to the Dutch West Indies with the permission of the English East India Company, but in reality, he was gathering intel on the local pirates and even managed to convince a few of them to take pardons and reform. He proposed a solution of turning Madagascar into a colony, but the EIC turned it down, deeming it dangerous for business. With that in mind, Rogers turned his attention to the Caribbean. The Crown supported his endeavors, mainly because it didn't have to spend nearly as much as it would on colonizing Madagascar. Rogers was given the title "Captain-General and Governor-in-Chief of the Bahamas," a title that came with no salary. More importantly, he was given permission to pardon pirates for any crimes they had committed prior to January 5th, 1718, as long as the pirates themselves surrendered to him.

When he arrived in the Caribbean, Rogers set out to establish his authority among the brutes that inhabited the islands, especially those of New Providence and its main town, Nassau. Rogers's plan was threefold:

1. Establish his reputation as governor and show himself as the main locus of power

2.Allow the pirates to do as they pleased as long as they did not commit open acts of piracy while ashore

3.Grant pardons to and convert at least several pirates while in office.

Rogers worked tirelessly while he was the governor of the Bahamas. He managed to build himself a fort and reinforce it in case of attacks from other nations. Furthermore, he established a basic system of governance on the island, with both his own associates and some of the local brutes serving in high positions. Next, he strived to turn Nassau and other shantytowns into places with decent living conditions, complete with roads, wells, workable fields, etc. However, not everything went according to plan. The year 1718 would prove to be a trying one for Rogers, as plague broke out on the island while Spanish galleons loomed in the waters. Furthermore, Charles Vane was still at large, and the notorious pirate had sworn vengeance upon Rogers, who had little means of defending himself. Rogers did manage to convert Benjamin Hornigold and another pirate to his cause by that point, but he still had an unfinished fort to complete and few ships with which to defend the island, an island that was full of pirates who were about as loyal as they were sober. In fact, during one desperate mission, Rogers sent two ships to get supplies from Hispaniola. The pirates on board those ships refused to return. Hornigold was dispatched to find them, which he did—they were severely mauled by the Spanish, with only thirteen men surviving and three of the survivors being mortally wounded. Hornigold took them back to Rogers, who then decided to do what was tantamount to a potentially suicidal task: he would hold court over the traitors in the open, in front of all the pirates on the island. In other words, he was about to invoke English law in the most lawless place possible, surrounded by people who could gun him down without batting an eye.

However, Rogers was undeterred. He held court over the traitors and sentenced them all to a public hanging, which occurred several days later in the open view of everyone. Surprisingly, not a single pirate went after Rogers, and they all watched the proceedings quietly. Rogers was effectively proving to the pirates that he was, indeed, the authority on the island and that his rock-solid unwavering nature represented England itself and her willingness to do away with the pirate menace. Some pirates did hatch an assassination plan, but Rogers caught wind of that through an informant and flogged them all publicly. Shockingly, he let them go afterward. This tactic was to show the pirates that such petty attempts at assassination were beneath him and that he had far more important work to do, thus cementing his authority on the island.

The following months were just as harsh, with Rogers working hard on building his fort while keeping the pirates pacified. He did so by providing them with alcohol and food, which, coupled with his open acts of authority against anyone who spoke out against him, proved to be a decent strategy. In early 1720, the Spanish came to Nassau, ready to go against the English, but at that point, Rogers was ready. The past year, the Crown had extended the royal pardon to all of the Caribbean pirates, which enabled Rogers to enlist the help of many other sea brigands. Of course, he did not provide privateering licenses to all of the pirates who accepted the pardon— Calico Jack, for instance, was refused a license—which was prudent on his part since Rogers could discern which former pirate captains would serve him well and which ones would not. Since Rackham went back to his piratical ways shortly after escaping with Anne Bonny, Rogers's strategy had again proven prudent. Either way, with the pirates now receiving pardons en masse, Rogers could count on several small fleets to defend New Providence from the Spanish, and indeed, the mere presence of these ships made the Spanish vessels turn tail.

In November of that same year, Calico Jack, the last of the notorious pirates of the Caribbean, would meet his end with a quick drop and a sudden stop. It was an impossible task, but Rogers managed to quell the pirate threat in the Caribbean and sow the seeds for a new colony on New Providence. His fort stood strong, the pirates were in disarray and hunting each other, and any outside menace was handled. However, Rogers would not enjoy the fruits of his success; throughout his tenure as governor, he had paid for everything in Nassau out of his own pocket, with his pleas for further financing from the Crown going unanswered. When he finally had enough, he sailed back to England in March, where he learned that the government was not ready or willing to compensate for his expenses in the new colony. He fell into a debtor's prison, once again declaring bankruptcy, and a new governor was sent in his place.

Over the next year or so, Rogers would stay in prison, but he continued to press his case with the authorities. Thanks to his friends and to him selling more of his property, he managed to pull himself out of debt, though he was still not entirely well with his health, and his honor had not yet been fully restored. Then, as if by fate, several events saw Rogers get what he deserved. Firstly, the army provided him with the rank of an infantry general, enabling him to earn half of a general's salary. Next, an author approached him to collect information about an upcoming book, which would prove to be a massive bestseller, as we will see in the upcoming chapters. This happened at some point before 1724. When that book was published, Rogers immediately saw a resurgence of support from everyone, including King George I himself. The king provided Rogers with compensation of his previous salary, all the way to 1721, but his successor, King George II, went one step further and appointed Rogers as the governor of the Bahamas once more in 1728.

During that same year, Rogers reunited with Sarah and his family, and they would go back to the same place he had helped pacify. Nassau was now a peaceful colonial plantation city, with a few more shanties left here and there. The only pirates present were retired old sea dogs who would still talk about the good old days of the sweet trade but who had little real interest in going back to it. The tiny fort Rogers had so much trouble building and fortifying now stood strong, protecting the island and the waters around it. But best of all was the official colonial seal that Rogers was presented with upon his return to Nassau, which bore an inscription in Latin that read *Expulsis Piratis, Restituta Commercia*, meaning "Pirates Expelled, Commerce Restored." It also bore an image of pirate vessels retreating, an accurate representation of everything Rogers had done for the Bahamas. And indeed, his legacy would last well beyond his death, with the colonial seal inscription serving as the official motto of the Bahamas until the islands became an independent nation in 1973.

Rogers died on July 15th, 1732; he was roughly fifty-three years old and in poor health. Much like Robert Maynard, he was a man whose greatest efforts in subduing the pirate threat didn't always find favor with the men at the top. However, his contribution to ending the Golden Age of Piracy is truly one for the history books.

The End of Prominent Sea Captains

Some scholars tend to cap off the Golden Age of Piracy with the year 1726. In that year, a minor pirate, William Fly, was hanged in Boston. And indeed, by the time Fly was raiding the high seas, most charismatic captains and pirates in general were either dead, had disappeared, or took advantage of their pardons and turned to privateering or even pirate hunting. A lot of these deaths were by hanging, a fate that was met by Calico Jack, the "Gentleman Pirate" Stede Bonnet, and the cruel Charles Vane. Others met their end during battle, like Blackbeard, Davis, and Black Bart. Quite a few died while in captivity, including Mary Read and her child. But not a single one of them managed to live out their lives with their riches intact and with the law not being on their heels. The Golden Age had proven that piracy might be a lucrative and often rewarding trade, but it was one that doomed people to their deaths from the very outset.

Another interesting detail of note is the fact that few pirates lived past forty, including retired or reformed ones. Blackbeard was roughly forty when he met his match, but the vast majority of pirates who were not captains were usually young men, anywhere between fifteen and twenty. Moreover, if you managed to survive for over three years while engaging in the sweet trade, you were one in hundreds of thousands to do so, as most pirates barely made it past their first month on a ship. Pirate captains themselves averaged about a year or a year and a half of activity, at most. Black Bart's motto of a merry yet short life seems to have been accurate, considering how few of his brothers in arms actually managed to live to old age. And let's not forget that there were no real prospects for former pirates that were as lucrative or as liberating as being on the open sea and plundering cargo from wealthy unsuspecting ships. Even privateers had to give a percentage of their loot to the Crown; otherwise, they would suffer legal repercussions. Indeed, engaging in the sweet trade was a short-lived pleasure that was inevitably succeeded by a gruesome end, as most of the men who made up the Golden Age came to find out.

Woodes Rogers *[right]* and his family *by William Hogarth, 1729, National Maritime Museum*

https://commons.wikimedia.org/wiki/File:Rogers,Woodes.jpg

Chapter 5 – Life at Sea: Typical Activities Aboard the Pirate Ship, the Pirate Look, the Pirate Code, On-Deck Atmosphere

Typical Activities Aboard the Pirate Ship

For years, Hollywood and entertainment in general have provided a highly romanticized image of pirates, and we will cover most of the particularities in the following chapter. Possibly the most prevalent one was the daily life of a regular pirate aboard a vessel being an exciting and testosterone-fueled affair, with scurvy dogs gambling, going after each other's throats, or singing sea shanties while their captain stared off into the distance, pondering on his next target. And as bizarre as the next sentence might seem, one of the most accurate depictions of a typical pirate crew's day was shown in the opening episodes of *Space Pirate Captain Harlock*, an anime adaptation of the science fiction manga of the same name created by Japanese author Leiji Matsumoto. In the show, we see pirates lazing around their massive spaceship, sleeping, or generally having fun, with the titular captain Harlock himself rarely forcing them to do anything. However, the minute danger strikes, the entire crew springs into action, and Harlock takes command, front and center.

But before we delve into what a regular day was for a pirate, we first need to address how a pirate ship operated and how people got involved in the sweet trade to begin with. Pirate ships rarely recruited sailors in a similar manner to the Royal Navy or a privateer; indeed, the majority of people would join pirates either willingly (after their vessel had been raided and plundered) or by force. And even then, a pirate ship was not going to pick up just anyone. You had to be a skilled sailor with at least a basic knowledge of seafaring to be spared or invited aboard. Other people were either left on board the plundered ship or set adrift.

Like other ships at the time, a pirate vessel had a simple hierarchy, though it wasn't as enforced as it might have been on an official ship of the navy. Starting from the top, there was the captain. His command was only absolute during a raid or a fighting engagement. At that point, he had complete control, and disobeying him would have been considered an offense. However, while on board the ship, the captain really was no different than any other pirate. For instance, regular pirates could freely walk into the captain's cabin and use it at their leisure. Captains could also be removed via a majority vote, from the most brutal like Charles Vane to the kindest like Edward England.

The ship's second most important person was the quartermaster. He was usually in charge of the day-to-day duties on board the ship, including the division of plunder and settling of petty disputes; he even doled out some of the punishments himself. Quartermasters, like captains (in most cases, at least), had to be literate and had to know at least basic mathematics in order to divide the spoils properly and maintain the ship's log. Frequently, quartermasters of one ship would become captains of another if a mutiny were to take place.

Boatswain, or bosun, was the next in line, and his job was to keep track of what the ship needed. He would look after the wood, the ropes, and the canvas for sails, and he often would go ashore with the crew and look for materials for repairs or supplies for restocking. He also oversaw the anchor dropping (and raising) and maintained the deck and the sails. Considering he was one of two men who kept the ship in good shape, a boatswain was an incredibly valuable member of the crew. Another member of equal importance was the carpenter, whose task was to perform repairs on the ship while at sea. He reported directly to the boatswain and had to do most of the grunt work regarding filling holes, keeping the mast in good shape, etc. On rare occasions, he would also perform the duties of a surgeon if a surgeon could not be found.

And speaking of, a surgeon was incredibly vital to any crew. In fact, they were so vital that anytime a pirate ship raided a vessel, they would recruit that vessel's surgeon by force. Injuries and diseases were frequent on every voyage, so a person well-versed in the medical arts (or handy with a saw if a limb needed to be cut) was a valuable asset. Of equal value was the ship's navigator. While a skilled captain would usually be able to navigate the ship himself, he would never turn down a crew member who was skilled in reading maps and keeping the ship on the right track. Much like surgeons, navigators were also often recruited against their will.

All ships had guns, and maintaining those guns was the job of a gunner. He would keep the guns in battle-ready shape, as well as take care of the gunpowder and other related items. Usually, a gunner was assisted by several young boys who carried powder to the cannons during a fight, earning them the unfortunate nickname "powder monkeys." Every single gunner in pirate history started off as a powder monkey at some point.

The last member of the crew who was more than a mere pirate was the musician. As odd as this might sound, a musician was as important to the pirate crew as the gunner or even the boatswain. Musicians kept the pirates entertained during long, dull voyages across the ocean and kept their spirits up in harsh times. And like surgeons and navigators, they almost exclusively joined pirate crews after being forced to do so.

Now we know who made up a typical pirate crew. So, what was a typical day for these men like? Well, unless they were in the middle of a raid or ashore drinking themselves to a stupor, their life at sea was incredibly mundane. As stated, most of these men were skilled sailors, and just like any other sailor, their entire time on deck was filled with them working around the ship and keeping it from sinking. They would hoist sails, raise or lower anchors, steer the vessel, tighten or loosen ropes, clean the deck, fish, do minor repairs, or none of the above. It was a dreadful existence, one that these men knew full well even before joining a pirate crew. Fresh food and water were luxuries on the open seas, and most pirates had to settle for stuff like salted beef, crackers, fish, or similar provisions. These provisions would almost always go bad during the journey. And yes, the pirates still had to eat the rotten food, considering they had no choice in the matter—the captain very much included. The crew all slept together, with their body odor and the stench of the sea quite prevalent. Bathing was definitely not an option until they reached shore. That's why it was no coincidence that scurvy and other diseases often struck ships, resulting in thousands of pirates dying without even seeing any action.

The Pirate Look

Pirates of legend tend to be colorful individuals with scarves tied behind their heads, hooks for hands, eyepatches, peglegs, long flowing coats, Cavalier boots, tricorn hats with feathers in them, and parrots on their shoulders. It might come as a surprise to learn, then, that nearly none of these were typical or even common pirate garments of the era. In fact, pirates dressed more or less the same as typical sailors of the time, and in the vast majority of cases, their garb was nothing to write home about.

A regular pirate's outfit consisted of either a narrow band-collared shirt or a sleeved waistcoat on the upper body and either trousers or wide-legged petticoat breeches on the lower body. They would usually cover their head with either a simple leather cap, a knitted Monmouth cap, a cloth cap that was trimmed with fur (some captains preferred this cap), or a low-crowned hat with a narrow brim. If the weather was cold, a pirate would wear a long woolen smock and a pair of knitted gloves or even mittens. Contrary to popular belief, pirates did not wear Cavalier boots, as they would be incredibly cumbersome during a raid, so they either went barefoot or, especially during the winter months or while going ashore, wore round-toe shoes with small buckles over stockings that were held up by tied garters.

Captains might choose to dress with a bit more flair, copying the maritime officers of the age. For instance, his upper body would be bedecked in a moderately long waistcoat, held tight by a short sash, and with a sleeved waistcoat of harder material that went up to his knees. His lower body would be dressed in breeches of higher quality than those of his crew, and he would wear fashionable shoes, albeit not as deep or square as is often depicted in fiction. Very few captains wore tricorn hats or put feathers in them, as tricorn hats would be incredibly cumbersome and could even impair a captain's vision. And speaking of head garments, the captain's crew rarely wore scarves on their heads, and even if they did, they usually tied them at the front, not the back. Finally, when it comes to peglegs and eyepatches, only pirates who lost limbs or eyes in battle would wear those, which did happen quite a bit.

Naturally, the key aspect of a pirate's look is his accent. And despite what fiction has given us in the past century and a half, there was no discernible pirate accent. In other words, it's highly unlikely that a pirate said, "Shiver me timbers!" or "Avast there, maties!" It is also not likely that a pirate grunted, "Arr!" Most pirates simply spoke with the dialect of their birthplace or their last place of residence. Blackbeard, for example, almost certainly spoke with an upper-class accent, considering where he was from and the fact that he was literate and a recreational reader. Some pirates, like Davis and Roberts, were bilingual or even multilingual, which helped when they wanted to register as privateers aboard vessels of countries other than their own.

Calico Jack Rackham, engraving from the original English edition of Captain Charles Johnson's A General History of the Pyrates, 18ᵗʰ Century

https://commons.wikimedia.org/wiki/File:Rackham,_Jack.jpg

The Pirate Code

As disorganized as pirates could be, at least in comparison to lawful naval officers of the time, they still operated under a set of rules. Each crew had a particular code that they had to follow, which varied from captain to captain, sometimes even varying from one voyage to the next. Such a document was called a pirate article or, more commonly, a pirate code.

There are several such codes preserved from historical documents, with probably the most famous one being that of Black Bart. His article contained eleven sections, and they went as follows:

1. Every crew member has the right to vote regarding the affairs of the moment. He is entitled to an equal share of fresh provisions, as well as strong liquor, to use as he pleases unless necessity and scarcity dictate that the provisions be

shared.

2. Every crew member is to be called fairly in turn, by list, on board of prizes. Aside from their proper share of the loot, they are allowed a change of clothes. However, if they defraud the company to the value of one dollar in jewels, plate, or money, they are to be marooned as a punishment. If a robbery took place between two crew members, the guilty party is to have his ears and nose slit, then be left in an inhabited place to encounter hardships.

3. No man is to gamble with cards or dice for money on board.

4. All lights and candles are going off at 8 o'clock at night. If any man wants to drink after that, they will do it on the open deck.

5. Every man is to clean his pistol and cutlass so it is ready for action.

6. No woman or young boy is to be allowed on board, and if any man is discovered to be seducing them or taking them to sea in disguise, their punishment is death.

7. Ship desertion or abandoning the post mid-battle is punishable by either death or marooning.

8. Nobody is allowed to fight on board. Any and all differences are to be settled onshore via a duel.

9. No man is to break their way of living until they have shared 1000 pounds. If a man loses his limb or becomes a cripple while in service, he will receive 800 pounds from the public stock and a proportional amount for any lesser injuries.

10. Of the loot, the captain and the quartermaster receive two shares; the master, boatswain, and gunner each receive a share and a half; and the other officers receive a share and a quarter.

11. Musicians are allowed to rest on the Sabbath Day, but they are required to work all six of the other days and nights unless they receive a special favor.

Most other pirate codes contain similar sections that generally deal with splitting the loot, ship responsibilities, or settling disputes.

Every time a new member was recruited, the senior officers (usually the captain or the quartermaster) would present them with the code and ask them to sign it. Then the pirate would have to swear to abide by the article, usually on a copy of the Bible. These rules applied to every single member of the crew, including the captain. In other words, the ability to vote the captain out of his position was not just a frequent occurrence; it was pretty much a requirement if the need arose.

These articles are often used by some historians to show that pirates created a de facto democratic society on board their ships. And while there's some truth to that, a pirate ship was far from a liberal democratic society where everyone got their say in the matter. For example, young officers and new crew members, usually powder monkeys, had very little say in the everyday matters of the voyage and were usually ignored by the senior members. Furthermore, both current and former slaves, if they found their way on board a pirate vessel, also had no say in any matters. As far as democracies go, these ships were not that different from any other corner of the planet in the late 17th and early 18th centuries.

More importantly, the ships were nowhere near as "independent" from their native country as people might think. There were definitely pirates who went against authority, but by and large, they were loyal to the country from which they originated. Benjamin Hornigold, for example, refused to attack English ships, partly to preserve his guise of a privateer but mostly because he was genuinely a patriot in a sense (which goes some way into explaining his loyalty to Woodes Rogers during his first term as governor).

On-Deck Atmosphere

As outlined earlier, life aboard a pirate ship was largely uneventful. When they were not busying about with the ship's affairs, the pirates on board would either drink excessively, sleep for hours, or laze around doing nothing in particular. Musicians helped pass the time, sure, but their music made little headway in quelling the many issues that a pirate might face on the open sea. Problems were aplenty, whether it was two pirates fighting over a mundane issue or a crew member stealing an extra ration of food. Each crime had a suitable punishment, and they were usually carried out by most of the crew or the quartermaster himself. Captains would dole out punishments too, but real brutalities, like those of Charles Vane, were rare.

By far, the most prominent punishment was marooning, where the belligerent(s) would be left on a desert island to fend for themselves. This was a common penalty for mutineers and seditionists, but a wide range of crimes could be punished by marooning if the captain and crew deemed it necessary. Of course, this punishment was not the most brutal. That dishonor goes to the act known as keelhauling. The pirate who committed a crime would be stripped naked and tied to a rope, with the rope then pulled underwater from one side of the ship to the next under the ship's keel (the bottom part of the ship, i.e., the structural element that stretches down the ship's whole length). Sailors would then drag the rope with the pirate underwater, pulling him back and forth. One of several things could happen next. Either he would drown, the rope would break and drag him under the ship, or his skin could be lacerated and slashed by the barnacles that grew on the keel, which were as sharp as razors. Most monstrously of all, if the pirate survived this absolute torture, the captain could order the crew to do the whole process all over again.

Some of the other punishments included tying a pirate to the mast and leaving him to suffer against the elements, selling him into slavery, dunking him in the water over and over again from the yard ram, flogging him with a whip called the cat o' nine tails, being clapped in irons, getting tossed overboard, or getting a rope tied around his eyes with someone tightening it until both eyeballs popped out (a practice known as woolding). Interestingly, walking the plank, although incredibly popular as part of pirate lore, was extremely rare and not particularly efficient. In fact, one of the only instances of recorded plank-walking among pirates happened in the 19th century, decades after the last pirate captain from the Golden Age met his end.

Chapter 6 – Myth vs. Fact: The Growth and Expansion of the Romanticized Pirate, Early Written Works on the Subject, Modern Misinterpretations of the Golden Age

Early Written Works on Piracy

Unfortunately, the life of a pirate was not particularly well documented back in the day, mainly because of the nature of the trade and the fact that few men were interested in the subject. However, once the first comprehensive written works on the subject of piracy came out, they captured the imagination of thousands of people from all walks of life. The problem with these accounts is that they tend to play fast and loose with facts, opting to sometimes invent entire sections whole-cloth purely to sensationalize the sweet trade and sell more copies. It was a great marketing tool, indeed, but it further complicated all later attempts at studying piracy from an objective, historical point of view.

Two works, in particular, had a profound effect on popularizing piracy. The first was written in Dutch by a former French buccaneer called Alexandre Exquemelin, and it bore the title *De Americaensche zee-roovers* (*The American Pirates*). Originally published in 1678, it went on to reach international fame through its translations in German, English, French, and Spanish. The book covered the lives and exploits of 17th-century buccaneers, but it had an air of authenticity to it, considering that Exquemelin was himself a member of several buccaneer crews, most notably that of Henry Morgan. The illustrations of the many pirates he described, including Roche Braziliano, François L'Olonnais, Henry Morgan, and Bartolomeu Português, proved especially engaging, so much so that the original copperplates of these pirates' portraits were bought and reused by printers all over Europe. Eventually, they wore out and had to be reengraved over and over again. The books sold immensely well, earning Exquemelin fame and a decent amount of money.

However, not everyone was pleased with this tome. Henry Morgan, in particular, took umbrage with it. He successfully sued the English publishers of the book, demanding that some sections of it be retracted (for instance, the ones where he supposedly used nuns and innocent locals as human shields during his capture of the third castle of Portobello in 1668). The publishers compensated him with £200, and all subsequent editions of the book retracted the sections in question.

While Exquemelin's 1678 book has proven that there was definitely a market out there for books on piracy, another author's work would skyrocket piracy into fame (or rather infamy). This author is still unknown to historians (some speculate it was Daniel Defoe using a pseudonym), but he went under the alias of Captain Charles Johnson. His work, *A General History of the Robberies and Murders of the most notorious Pyrates*, was published in 1724, and it contained biographies of twenty-one different pirates, including the most famous names like Blackbeard, Stede Bonnet, Calico Jack, and Black Bart. However, while the men and women mentioned in his book did exist historically, he took a considerable creative license when it came to their appearance, dialogue, and overall events in which they took part. For example, this tome would be the first to describe Black Bart's lavish outfit, as well as his dramatic death on deck during a fight. Furthermore, he would ascribe famous words to Anne Bonny while she and Jack were in captivity; namely, before Jack was about to be executed, he spoke to her in prison, and she told him, "I am sorry to see you here, Jack, but if you had fought like a man, you would not be hanged like a dog." Johnson's most famous inventions found their place in Blackbeard's biography. Some choice examples include the following:

- Blackbeard once shot a crew member out of nowhere. When asked by his crew why he did it, he simply said, "If I don't kill someone now and then, you'll forget who I am."

- At one point, he said to his crew, "Let us make a hell of our own and try how long we can bear it," and they all went down the ship's hold. He closed the hatches, filled a few pots with brimstone, and set them on fire, engulfing the room in sulfurous fumes. All of the men started suffocating and rushed out, but Blackbeard remained and came out last.

- Evidently, a dark figure would often appear on board Blackbeard's ship. Pirates assumed that it was the Devil himself, keeping an eye on Blackbeard.

- Blackbeard evidently married an underage girl after accepting his pardon, then had his men take turns raping her after he had his own way with her.

- Though not without basis in reality, the famous "Damn you for Villains, who are you?" exchange between Blackbeard and Maynard was definitely an embellishment on Johnson's part.

Johnson's book was rife with inaccuracies, but that didn't stop the public from buying it en masse. It was so popular, in fact, that a second expanded volume was published in 1726. There's no denying that the fascination with pirates in the coming centuries, one that lasts to this very day, originated with Johnson's book. Whoever he may have been, he was definitely responsible for creating and promoting the modern conception of pirates, much more than Exquemelin did over half a century prior.

The Growth and Expansion of the Romanticized Pirate

Both *The American Pirates* and *A General History of the Robberies and Murders of the most notorious Pyrates* were, for a long time, the only authoritative sources on contemporary and past piracy. As such, they served as an inspiration to many great fiction authors who chose to include piracy, either as a central motif or as an element. Robert Louis Stevenson's famous work *Treasure Island* actually drew inspiration from Johnson's book, with Stevenson himself openly stating that the work had a profound influence on him. The same book went on to influence Sir James Matthew (J. M.) Barrie, the author of *Peter Pan*, who crafted his villainous Captain Hook based on the pirates described by Johnson. Some of the most prominent pirate tropes, such as the eyepatch, the parrot, the pegleg, and the act of burying treasure, found their way into the public consciousness directly from *Treasure Island* itself. In addition, once cinema had become a new and popular art form, a 1950 Disney adaptation of *Treasure Island* saw the first instance of the infamous "pirate accent"; actor Robert Newton, who portrayed Long John Silver, spoke with an exaggerated West Country English accent, and due to the popularity of the film, said accent became engraved in popular culture and remains linked to pirates to this day.

Quite a few myths related to piracy also came out of Hollywood, especially the swashbuckling aspect of a dashing pirate captain brandishing a rapier and swinging from ship to ship. In reality, most pirate captains were equipped with cutlasses and pistols, and if they did wear flamboyant clothing as they did in films, they would be rendered useless in any real battle. The same can be said about prolonged battles between ships, with broadsides firing ammo at each other for hours. However, such battles at sea were rare. In fact, pirates generally avoided battle if they could since their main goal was to plunder valuables and sell them off. Fighting was done as the very last resort, and even then, it wasn't nearly as epic or long-lasting as Hollywood movies made it out to be. In fact, it was far more likely that pirates would retreat at the mere sight of a warship.

One of the most persistent myths that actually has some basis in fact is the infamous black flag, the Jolly Roger. Most of the flag designs given for various captains (Blackbeard, Thomas Tew, Edward England, Black Bart, etc.) were likely inventions by Johnson. However, pirates did raise flags when going after their target. For example, if they wanted to approach a vessel, they would raise the flag of any maritime nation, be it England, Spain, France, or any other. Once they got close enough, they would raise the black flag, letting people know that they were pirates and that they intended to board the ship. This was usually followed by a warning shot from a gun. However, if the other ship persisted and failed to surrender, pirates would raise the red flag, signaling that no quarter would be given to the other ship. Initially, pirates before and during the buccaneering period almost exclusively used the red flag; the practice of raising the black flag emerged somewhere around the War of the Spanish Succession.

Finally, there's the prevailing myth of pirates burying their treasure. Save for a few scarce examples of questionable authenticity (Captain Kidd, David Marteen, and James Plantain), pirates never buried anything. In fact, burying one's treasure would be counterproductive at best; one of the crew members could simply mutiny and find the treasure, then unearth it for himself. Furthermore, there was always a danger of someone else finding the loot and picking it up. In reality, pirates almost always sold their loot, which hardly ever consisted of huge chests of gold, silver, and diamonds, as shown in movies. Such chests would be incredibly heavy for even two people to carry, even without the precious cargo in them. Pirates actually stole a wide variety of items, including fabrics, spices, herbs, food, liquor, charts and maps, tobacco, instruments, weaponry, clothing, and even ornamental items.

A few myths also came out of the somewhat flawed view of early historians and intellectuals. Prominent left-leaning critics, largely adherents of communism and socialism, would often proclaim that piracy was the precursor to democracy and social justice, that the average pirate freed the slaves, that there was no racism or prejudice aboard a pirate ship, and that they were liberators who stood against oppressive governments. And while it is true that pirates had no love for authority and that they would often free slaves, they were far from being paragons of virtue. A pirate's main goal was and always will be profit, and more often than not, they would simply resell the liberated pirates or maroon them somewhere. True, some slaves did join the crew, but that didn't make the pirates any more or less tolerant than any other person of the age. In fact, some pirates would even go as far as to buy slaves from native African slaveowners of the West African coast and then capture the slaveowners themselves and put them in chains. (Slavery was already booming on the African continent shortly after the Europeans set up factories along the coastline, and the local chieftains were earning insane amounts of money from selling slaves.) If a pirate ship ran into a slave-carrying vessel, they would capture it and then ransom it back to the captain or the company for a hefty sum, making the slaves a simple bargaining chip.

In terms of modern leftist ideas, some scholars even champion pirates as the early acceptors of homosexuality, considering that they allowed no women on board and that some sources spoke of pirate captains abstaining from sex and even having male lovers. (Johnson's book claims that Black Bart had a male lover on board, but that was more than likely another one of the author's many sensational inventions; Roberts was indeed abstinent, but that was due to his strong Christian beliefs and his sense of discipline.) There is a very strong possibility that at least some of the men on pirate crews had homosexual leanings, though none of it has been recorded, so we don't know the extent of this phenomenon one way or the other. Furthermore, as we saw with Roberts's pirate code, people who practiced sodomy were subject to harsh punishment. Usually, that would entail being marooned on a desert island with one's suspected partner, and oftentimes, they were left with a pistol or a knife in order to take their own life if they so chose. Similar punishments were also in place if a pirate were to sneak a woman on board. Rackham's crew had two women employed, but he was the exception to the rule; in other words, pirates were hardly champions of women's rights, and the same could be said about racial and sexual equality. As always, a pirate's goal was to get loot, and saving slaves or canoodling with people of either sex was a detriment to that.

Interestingly, one myth that was heavily steeped in fact was the infamous pirate binge drinking. Nearly all pirates were heavy drunkards (with notable exceptions like Black Bart), considering that there weren't too many things to do on board a pirate ship. What's more, some documented raids from the time saw Benjamin Hornigold and Blackbeard specifically raiding a ship to take its liquor, leaving everything else behind (except for hats; apparently, they were indulging in some heavy drinking the night before and threw their hats overboard in a drunken state). Pirates would drink just as heavily onshore, a detail that helped Woodes Rogers keep them in check during his first stint as the governor of the Bahamas.

Ultimately, there were both positive and negative points to being a pirate when compared to regular naval work. Pirates did have more freedom than regular sailors since they did not have to suffer under their captain's yoke. On the other hand, the captain of a naval ship was the supreme authority and was not to be questioned, much to the chagrin of the crew. However, pirates were largely undisciplined fighters, as we've seen above. In contrast, English commanders who ran the ships were experienced, battle-hardened men and fierce tacticians with utmost discipline, meaning they were well-equipped for battle. That was one of the main reasons why pirates generally avoided fighting, as they knew there would be a good chance they would be soundly defeated. That's why Lieutenant Maynard, though a much shorter and less intimidating man than Blackbeard, chose to fight him one-on-one and why his crew ultimately came out victorious. As liberating as it was to be a pirate, it didn't teach one discipline or proper warfare on the open sea; at most, it taught a person how to be an expert plunderer and how to successfully flee from danger (although the success of those escapes was shoddy and short-lived at the best of times).

Yet, despite all of the dangers that ultimately came with the sweet trade, people still willingly, for the most part, chose to be pirates. They were ready to risk losing a limb or, worse yet, losing their life for the simple reason of being able to drink whenever they wanted, eat whenever they wanted, sleep whenever they wanted, and be as wanton and as lecherous as their pocketbook allowed them to be. It was a form of freedom few free men of low status experienced, and this fact ultimately attracted people to piracy the most.

Bartholomew Roberts's crew drinking from The Pirates Own Book by Charles Ellms, 1837

Chapter 7 – After the Golden Age: Piracy and Maritime Law Enforcement

The mid- and late 1720s were not particularly active when it comes to piracy. The last pirate of note to be executed was not even particularly notorious, and the high seas were a proverbial wasteland. Of course, piracy never really ceased, but its frequency went down significantly, and the Golden Age was pretty much over. Even if the few surviving pirates didn't call it by that name, they knew that the end had come. The question is, what made this particular decade, i.e., the 1720s in general, the nadir of the sweet trade?

Generally speaking, we can break the end of the Golden Age down into five parts that correspond to the different events that affected it. First and foremost, the deaths of prominent pirates all took place roughly between 1717 and 1726, sometimes mere months apart from each other. The death of Bartholomew Roberts, the last of the extremely notorious pirates, in 1722 might not have moved too many people to reconsider pirating, but the gruesome end that his crew met at the hands of the authorities certainly roused a few men. Of course, their deaths were far from being the only public displays of anti-piracy justice that the men of the Caribbean and beyond saw. Pirates that sailed with Henry Every, Calico Jack,

Stede Bonnet, Charles Vane, and even William Kidd all met brutal demises at the hands of the law long before Black Bart's men even set sail. But with such a powerful pirate crew as that of Roberts being wiped out easily by the government (we should remember that Roberts captured hundreds of ships), some men most assuredly chose not to engage with maritime theft any longer.

The second prominent reason behind the end of the Golden Age is the disappearance of piratical safe havens, whose many bases were scattered around the Caribbean and the coast of Africa. Nassau had become a respectable town in a respectable colony thanks to Woodes Rogers, and Port Royal had been dismantled as a base long before the third period of the Golden Age even took off. On the other side of the globe, most of the bases on Madagascar were either destroyed or belonged to tribal kings, including Plantain himself, who wasn't really pirating all that often during that time. Ocracoke and the American coast were definitely off the table, with the island, in particular, becoming a notorious spot after Blackbeard's demise. Naturally, there were plenty of other illegal sites on the planet where pirates could have made their haven. Bases along the coasts of Brazil, South Africa, and Zanzibar and areas in the Gulf of Mexico were already rife with illegal activity. However, few pirates ever bothered to find their fortune in these places. Few would even try to trade there, despite some of these areas readily accepting contraband goods. And speaking of, a typical pirate could no longer sell stolen loot at American ports, largely because port towns fought against piracy by refusing to purchase anything that wasn't legally acquired. The pirates lost some of the most lucrative markets with that trade ban, which meant they couldn't even make their loot work for them in the rare event they stole some.

Of course, some events outside of the pirates' direct purview also affected the situation on the high seas. The third reason behind the ultimate end of the Golden Age was the Royal Navy's actual push to protect their waters from pirates. Some of the steps had been taken a lot earlier, with a few ships being sent to the Indian Ocean to patrol the waters and protect the East India Company's ships. But it was during the 1720s that such steps became more common. Each overseas governor petitioned the central government to send vessels to patrol their waters, and more often than not, they would employ reformed pirates as pirate hunters. This did not end piracy altogether, and for many more decades to come, lots of ships with rich cargo would sail the former pirate routes without protection. Nevertheless, the mere increased presence of navy ships deterred pirates from even trying anything, considering that no matter how equipped a pirate fleet was, it almost always avoided direct contact with navy vessels and men-of-war.

The fourth major reason concerns the conditions of everyday English sailors. As the 1720s pressed forward, the lot of a regular seaman greatly improved. For example, sailors were given regular pensions and compensated adequately with a solid salary increase. Furthermore, all sailors were provided with improved and mandated medical aid, making the profession just a smidgeon safer than it used to be. But most importantly, each sailor now had an incentive to avoid turning to piracy if he was unsatisfied with his service. In fact, the navy provided awards to any sailor who successfully resisted pirate attacks, meaning that seafarers would actively go out of their way to hunt for pirates for an added bonus. Of course, these changes were small steps toward a complete reformation of the navy, and the typical life aboard a naval ship was still a living hell for the most part, but it was still a step in the right direction nonetheless.

Finally, the fifth and final reason that contributed to the end of the Golden Age of Piracy was the birth of new ideas across Europe, those of freedom and individual human rights. While both the American and French Revolutions were still decades away, the ideas they would champion were already put into practice by lawmakers across the European continent. Capital punishment, for example, was no longer used for petty offenses and was reserved only for the gravest of crimes, while prisons and workhouses adopted more humane treatments. In addition, the elites were abolishing torture as a viable method of extracting information and turning to different, more effective methods.

In addition to this newfound loosening of the yoke of state authority, the little man could also enjoy a bit of personal freedom directly. The American settlers were now moving ever inward from the Atlantic coast, and new workable fields were discovered along the way that required more people to work them. As such, local governments encouraged more newcomers to settle and work the fields legally. So, instead of turning to piracy, everyday people simply migrated to America and started settling it by the thousands. It was a way for the common man to strike out on his own and live a free, secure life without authorities breathing down his neck. Furthermore, there was a clear financial incentive in striking out on your own in America and other settlements; you could earn money without worrying that someone might blow your arm off or cut you down, leaving you to bleed to death on the open sea, your body being tossed overboard and swallowed by the cold waves. Given the opportunity, even the most hardcore pirate would have chosen this kind of life, which was why quite a few of them turned to owning plantations and fields even during the height of the Golden Age (though, as we saw, they all eventually went back to their old trade, which cost them dearly).

Conclusion

Seven and a half decades is quite a long time for a trade to last, to thrive and expand, and to rise and fall. Few trades, illegal or otherwise, can have as rich of a history as piracy during its heyday, which wasn't called the "Golden Age" for nothing. Of course, it was almost nothing like it is described in popular fiction, nor did it look remotely like it is portrayed in famed Hollywood movies, but as they say, truth is stranger than fiction. After all, what's a more exciting story than that of hunters and meat smokers, of men with little maritime experience turning into some of the most feared sea brigands alive? How many stories contain a wannabe pirate who bought his way into illegality and paid the ultimate price for it? How many men can boast about capturing hundreds of ships and commanding the respect of drunks and brigands while barely taking a sip themselves? How many men can boast about arriving in an equivalent of a no man's land and turning it into a respectable colony with proper defenses and thriving trade? What man can boast about becoming a king of an entire island, an island that was larger than both his native and his motherland's island combined? And where can you find a better "tragedy of errors" than that of a privateer who turned pirate almost by accident, despite claiming otherwise? And indeed, what duel can outshine one between a stern, professional lieutenant and a massive, rowdy pirate who terrified the men around the American coast and the Caribbean? A duel that ultimately ended with a beheading and the birth of an absolute legend?

Make no mistake, the life of a pirate during the Golden Age of Piracy was far from glamorous or even exciting. These were harsh men bred to endure the terrifying conditions of seafaring life, people who risked life and limb to plunder massive quantities of loot and spend it all on drinking, whoring, and reveling until the waves called again. They were free, in a sense, but in another, they were not entirely different from any other people of the time. To some people, like Bonnet, Davis, Roberts, and Morgan, piracy was a way of life that they embraced with open arms. But to others, it was often the only viable option to make a living, which went some way to show just how grim the prospects of an everyman in 17th- and 18th-century Europe (or one of the European colonies) could be.

Indeed, stories of pirates were exaggerated and changed over the years, with details added and other details removed. Few pirates, if any, were swashbucklers like Errol Flynn's Captain Blood or charismatic losers like Johnny Depp's Jack Sparrow. Even fewer were as colorful and jolly as Monkey D. Luffy and his crew or as stoic and honorable as Captain Harlock. And sadly, none of them spoke with the same accent that Robert Newton made popular. There was no walking the plank, no treasure burying, no Libertatia (Republic of Pirates), no epic broadside cannonades on the open sea, or no tricorn hat-wearing, parrot-spotting, long-coat wearing, Cavalier boot-stomping captains who sailed gigantic ships with three masts. As all things tend to become over time, the sweet trade was made to look even sweeter through romanticizing, and impressionable authors would use limited information and their own imagination to build a cult. However, the only reason they did so in the first place is because of how powerful the pirate phenomenon had been. After all, these people, these notorious criminals, were all real-life historical personalities—from Laurens de Graaf and François L'Olonnais to Henry Morgan and Henry Every, from William Kidd and Charles Vane to Edward Teach and Jack Rackham, from Anne Bonny and Mary Read to James Plantain. They were all alive and active at some point, and they all had goals, aspirations, and dreams, as well as problems and setbacks. They were an inseparable part of everyday life during the 17th and 18th centuries, much like hackers and political activists are part of our own. And the fact that they managed to stir up such an uproar with their acts makes them all the more amazing, notwithstanding the fact that, at their core, they were criminals of ill repute who sometimes committed highly questionable or even downright despicable acts.

The Golden Age of Piracy is an inextricable part of our collective history, and as such, it should remain as an interesting, if a bit romantic, subject that deserves further research, but it also serves as a cautionary tale of what can happen when law breaks down and people get desperate. With the resurgence of piracy in some of the more destitute parts of the world, such as the Somalian coast and sections of the Indonesian archipelago, it's definitely worth considering how we handled piracy throughout history. In order to figure out how to stop the modern pirate problem, we need to look at how the issue was handled during the time when the sweet trade was the undisputed lord of the open seas.

Captain Kidd Burying His Treasure *by Howard Pyle, circa 1911*

https://commons.wikimedia.org/wiki/File:Pyle_pirates_burying2.jpg

Here's another book by Captivating History that you might like

HISTORY OF
COLONIAL AMERICA

A CAPTIVATING GUIDE TO THE COLONIAL HISTORY OF THE UNITED STATES, PURITANS, ANNE HUTCHINSON, THE PILGRIMS, MAYFLOWER, PEQUOT WAR, AND QUAKERS

CAPTIVATING HISTORY

Free Bonus from Captivating History (Available for a Limited time)

Hi History Lovers!

Now you have a chance to join our exclusive history list so you can get your first history ebook for free as well as discounts and a potential to get more history books for free! Simply visit the link below to join.

Captivatinghistory.com/ebook

Also, make sure to follow us on Facebook, Twitter and Youtube by searching for Captivating History.

Bibliography and References

McIntosh, Matthew (2020, June 2). *Caribbean Histories: Early Migration to Slavery to 20th-Century Transitions.* Brewminate. Retrieved September 8, 2022, from https://brewminate.com/caribbean-histories-early-migration-to-slavery-to-20th-century-transitions/

The American Revolution in the Caribbean: The untold story. Smithsonian Associates. (n.d.). Retrieved September 8, 2022, from https://smithsonianassociates.org/ticketing/tickets/american-revolution-in-caribbean-the-untold-story

Board, E., Studien, F. T., & Stiftung, M. W. (n.d.). *War and Revolution in the Caribbean – The Lesser Antilles, 1789–1815.* TRAFO. Retrieved September 8, 2022, from https://trafo.hypotheses.org/18614

Brief Histories: The Caribbean. Brief Histories: The Caribbean | Reviews in History. (n.d.). Retrieved September 8, 2022, from https://reviews.history.ac.uk/review/549

The British West Indies. The British Empire in The Caribbean: The British West Indies. (n.d.). Retrieved September 8, 2022, from https://www.britishempire.co.uk/maproom/caribbean.htm

Caribbean Theater of the American Revolutionary War. Military Wiki. (n.d.). Retrieved September 8, 2022, from https://military-history.fandom.com/wiki/Caribbean_theater_of_the_American_Revolutionary_War

Chen, C. P. (n.d.). *Caribbean Sea and Gulf of Mexico Campaigns.* WW2DB. Retrieved September 8, 2022, from https://ww2db.com/battle_spec.php?battle_id=276

Emmer, P. C., & Gommans, J. J. L. (n.d.). *The Caribbean (Chapter 4) - The Dutch Overseas Empire, 1600-1800*. Cambridge Core. Retrieved September 8, 2022, from https://www.cambridge.org/core/books/dutch-overseas-empire-16001800/caribbean/825DE672F0E6D7948FD8B8F740539D3E

Encyclopedia Britannica, inc. (n.d.). *2010 Haiti Earthquake*. Encyclopedia Britannica. Retrieved September 8, 2022, from https://www.britannica.com/event/2010-Haiti-earthquake

Encyclopedia Britannica, inc. (n.d.). *French Revolution*. Encyclopedia Britannica. Retrieved September 8, 2022, from https://www.britannica.com/event/French-Revolution

Europe in the Age of the Religious Wars, 1560-1575. Historyguide.org. (n.d.). Retrieved September 8, 2022, from http://www.historyguide.org/earlymod/lecture6c.html

European Wars of Religion. Military Wiki. (n.d.). Retrieved September 8, 2022, from https://military-history.fandom.com/wiki/European_wars_of_religion

Ferguson, J. (2020, May 5). *On the Home Front: World War I and the Caribbean*. Caribbean Beat Magazine. Retrieved September 8, 2022, from https://www.caribbean-beat.com/issue-128/home-front

France & French Collections at the Library of Congress: Americas & the Caribbean. Research Guides. (n.d.). Retrieved September 8, 2022, from https://guides.loc.gov/french-collections/francophone-studies/americas-caribbean

French and Dutch Settlements in North America. History for kids. (2020, April 27). Retrieved September 8, 2022, from https://www.historyforkids.net/american-history/new-explorers/french-and-dutch-settlements.html/

History Today | Published in History Today Volume 71 Issue 5 May 2021. (n.d.). *Is Caribbean History the Key to Understanding the Modern World?* History Today. Retrieved September 8, 2022, from https://www.historytoday.com/archive/head-head/caribbean-history-key-understanding-modern-world

History.com Editors. (2009, November 9). *French Revolution*. History.com. Retrieved September 8, 2022, from https://www.history.com/topics/france/french-revolution

Khan Academy. (n.d.). *French and Dutch Exploration in the New World*. Khan Academy. Retrieved September 8, 2022, from https://www.khanacademy.org/humanities/us-history/colonial-america/early-english-settlement/a/french-and-dutch-exploration

Magazine, S. (2009, October 1). *Columbus' Confusion about the New World*. Smithsonian.com. Retrieved September 8, 2022, from https://www.smithsonianmag.com/travel/columbus-confusion-about-the-new-world-140132422/

Magazine, S. (2011, October 1). *What Became of the Taino?* Smithsonian.com. Retrieved September 8, 2022, from https://www.smithsonianmag.com/travel/what-became-of-the-Taino-73824867/

McLean, J. (n.d.). *History of Western Civilization II*. French Explorers | History of Western Civilization II. Retrieved September 8, 2022, from https://courses.lumenlearning.com/suny-hccc-worldhistory2/chapter/french-explorers/

Minster, C. (2021, July 18). *Why Did the U.S. Military Occupy Haiti from 1915 to 1934?* ThoughtCo. Retrieved September 8, 2022, from https://www.thoughtco.com/haiti-the-us-occupation-1915-1934-2136374

Morris, W. B. B. G. (2021, October 8). *Dictatorship Masked as Democracy: A Timeline of the 1915 U.S. Invasion and Occupation of Haiti*. NewsOne. Retrieved September 8, 2022, from https://newsone.com/4214447/a-timeline-of-the-1915-u-s-invasion-and-occupation-of-haiti/

National Geographic Society. (2015, August 7). *The Dutch Influence in New Netherland*. National Geographic Society. Retrieved September 8, 2022, from https://www.nationalgeographic.org/activity/the-dutch-influence-in-new-netherland/

Pirates and Plantations: Exploring the Relationship between Caribbean Piracy and the Plantation Economy during the Early Modern Period. Tucaksegee Valley Historical Review. (n.d.). Retrieved September 8, 2022, from https://affiliate.wcu.edu/tuckasegeevalleyhistoricalreview/spring-2020/pirates-and-plantations-exploring-the-relationship-between-caribbean-piracy-and-the-plantation-economy-during-the-early-modern-period/

The Problem of Emancipation: The Caribbean Roots of the American Civil War. The Problem of Emancipation: The Caribbean Roots of the American Civil War | Department of African American Studies. (1970, January 1). Retrieved September 8, 2022, from https://afamstudies.yale.edu/publications/problem-emancipation-caribbean-roots-american-civil-war

Ransome, D. (n.d.). *World War One and the Caribbean*. Caribbean Intelligence. Retrieved September 8, 2022, from https://www.caribbeanintelligence.com/content/world-war-one-and-caribbean

Ronald Reagan on the Caribbean! Grasping Reality by Brad DeLong. (n.d.). Retrieved September 8, 2022, from https://delong.typepad.com/sdj/2007/06/ronald-reagan-5.html

Rotton, T. (2022, June 9). *2021 Haiti Earthquake and Tropical Storm Grace*. Center for Disaster Philanthropy. Retrieved September 8, 2022, from https://disasterphilanthropy.org/disasters/2021-haiti-earthquake-and-tropical-storm-grace/

Shaw, M. (2013, September 9). *The Trent Affair*. The British Library - The British Library. Retrieved September 8, 2022, from https://www.bl.uk/onlinegallery/onlineex/uscivilwar/britain/trentaffair/trentaffair.html

A Spotlight on a Primary Source by Christopher Columbus. (n.d.). *Columbus Reports on His First Voyage*. Columbus reports on his first voyage, 1493 | Gilder Lehrman Institute of American History. Retrieved September 8, 2022, from https://www.gilderlehrman.org/history-resources/spotlight-primary-source/columbus-reports-his-first-voyage-1493

U.S. Intervention in the Caribbean. New Articles RSS. (n.d.). Retrieved September 8, 2022, from https://encyclopedia.1914-1918-online.net/article/us_intervention_in_the_caribbean

Who Were the Real Pirates of the Caribbean? Royal Museums Greenwich. (n.d.). Retrieved September 8, 2022, from https://www.rmg.co.uk/stories/topics/who-were-real-pirates-caribbean

Bowling, T. (2008): *Pirates and Privateers*. Harpenden, UK: Pocket Essentials

Bromley, J. S. (1987): *Corsairs and Navies 1660-1760*. London, UK: The Hambledon Press

Encyclopedia Britannica (1981), Retrieved on August 19th 2021, from https://www.britannica.com

Golden Age of Piracy (2012), Retrieved on August 19th 2021, from https://goldenageofpiracy.org

Head, D. (Ed.) (2018): *The Golden Age of Piracy: The Rise, Fall, and Enduring Popularity of Pirates*. Athens, GA, USA: The University of Georgia Press

Konstam, A. (1998): *Pirates 1660-1730*. Oxford, UK: Osprey Publishing

Konstam, A. (2000): *Buccaneers*. Oxford, UK: Osprey Publishing

Konstam, A. (2007): *Scourge of the Seas: Buccaneers, Pirates and Privateers*. Oxford, UK: Osprey Publishing

Konstam, A. & Rickman, D. (2011): *Pirate: The Golden Age*. Oxford, UK: Osprey Publishing

Konstam, A. (2013): *Blackbeard's Last Fight: Pirate Hunting in North Carolina 1718*. Oxford, UK: Osprey Publishing

Konstam, A. (2016): *The Barbary Pirates 15th-17th Centuries*. Oxford, UK: Osprey Publishing

Little, B. (2016): *The Golden Age of Piracy: The Truth Behind Pirate Myths*. New York, NY, USA: Skyhorse Publishing

Lungsford, V. W. (2005): *Piracy and Privateering in the Golden Age Netherlands*. London, UK: Palgrave Macmillan

Montague, C. (2009): *Pirates and Privateers*. Eastbourne, UK: Canary Press

Rediker, M. (2004): *Villains of All Nations: Atlantic Pirates in the Golden Age*. Boston, MA, USA: Beacon Press

Sherry, F. (1986): *Raiders & Rebels: A History of the Golden Age of Piracy*. New York, NY, USA: HarperCollins

Tinniswood, A. (2010): *Pirates of Barbary: Corsairs, Conquests, and Captivity in the Seventeenth Century Mediterranean*. New York, NY, USA: Riverhead Books

Wikipedia (January 15, 2001), Retrieved on August 19th 2021, from www.wikipedia.org/

Made in the USA
Coppell, TX
23 January 2023

11556582R00125